Misadventures in Travel:

A Missionary's Experience in Brazil

Paula Edwards

HANNIBAL BOOKS
www.hannibalbooks.com

Published by
Hannibal Books
PO Box 461592
Garland, TX 75046-1592
Copyright Paula Edwards, 2010
All Rights Reserved
Printed in the United States of America
by Lightning Source, La Vergne, TN
Cover design by Dennis Davidson
Author photo on back cover by First Class Photo and Patrick Jelks

All Scripture taken from the Holy Bible,
New International Version, copyright 1973, 1978, 1984
by International Bible Society
ISBN 978-1-934749-79-1
Library of Congress Control Number 2010928180

TO ORDER ADDITIONAL COPIES SEE PAGE 191

Dedicated

to my husband,

Van,

who shared these experiences with me.
God inspired him
to go to Brazil in the first place.

Writing this story
took both of us.

What Others Are Saying about This Book:

Facing challenges daily as they travel in a foreign land, Paula and Van Edwards meet each challenge with faith in God for leadership and protection. Their story is moving as you find yourself believing you are traveling along highways and pothole-filled lanes in the Edwardses' often-"limping" vehicles. God's gracious provisions are so evident in each captivating chapter. A must-read for an up-to-date vision of today's missions and missionary life.

Bill Davis, founder and president
Church Starts International, Henrietta, TX

Paula Edwards' accounts of her and her husband Van's travels in Brazil with insight and humor illustrate how they depended on God to get them through some daunting situations while they mapped remote coastal areas for future church planting.

David Hodges, missionary to Brazil for more than 20 years
Director of the language school in Campinas, SP, Brazil, for more than seven years

I laughed. I cried. I felt called to be a missionary in Brazil—almost. *Misadventures in Travel* is a delightful excursion into the life and culture of Brazil as seen through the eyes of a daring guest. I recommend this book to anyone who enjoys a great adventure from the safety of an armchair.

Harry Black, associational missionary
Washington Madison Baptist Association, Fayetteville, AR

Paula Edwards has written a highly descriptive account of the Edwardses' experiences as short-term missionaries in Brazil. Paula is very expressive and funny; she makes one feel the situation of the Edwardses' travels. We certainly can be thankful how God does protect and help in our predicaments. We liked the last chapter's application of the road map and the Bible. Since we were missionaries in Brazil for 36 years, we could relate well to many events described.

Joe and Leona Tarry, retired missionaries to Brazil
International Mission Board, Southern Baptist Convention

Being confronted with challenges that range from being lost in the enormous sand dunes of northern Brazil to learning to communicate daily in another language became everyday occurrences for these adventuresome missionaries. Travel along with the Edwardses as they learn how God takes care of His children wherever they are.

Nolen and Sheilah Pridemore
(Nolen) IMB cluster strategy leader, Americas/Caribbean Diaspora
Former regional leader in Brazil

Each of us is on a journey. Often we fail to take the time to reflect and put on paper the activity of God in our lives. Follow Van and Paula Edwards on their journey to discover unreached people groups in the fishing villages of Brazil. You will laugh, smile, and be amazed at how God demonstrates His faithfulness, protection, and provision. You also will be encouraged to discover the many ways He works to help you navigate the journey of your own life.

Ronnie Toon, associational missionary
Independence Baptist Association, Batesville, AR

I have followed the Edwardses' *Misadventures* in my country, Brazil, and I have loved reading about them. From the perspective of a Brazilian I am pleased to see Paula and Van deal with their *Misadventures* in such a positive, funny, and enriching way. What a great way to get to know Brazil!

Pierre Coudry, director
Interclass Language School, Campinas, Brazil

Acknowledgements

I want to thank our daughters, Nancy and Marci, who were sad to see us leave for Brazil but who supported us all the way. Living without their parents nearby was a sacrifice.

I would like to acknowledge missionaries all over the world who have left home and family to daily take on the task of spreading the Good News to those who never have heard.

Thanks, also, to those who don't go but who do give to support missionaries on the field. Without such support no one could go.

I thank the International Mission Board missionaries in Brazil who helped us so much. I won't name names, but you know who you are.

Thanks to the many Brazilians who graciously helped us adjust to life in their country.

Most of all, I thank God for blessing us with the opportunity to serve Him in this way. I thank Him for giving us the health to accomplish the task and for His protection during our travels. Although our trucks were sick a lot, Van and I never even needed a bandage.

Contents

Foreword #1

One of the first steps in church planting is to determine the locations of places in which new churches are needed. This is a beautiful story of how one couple set out on a long journey to discover coastal fishing villages in need of churches from which the gospel can be proclaimed. Paula Edwards shares the numerous misadventures she and her husband, Van, experienced while they traveled the northeast coast of Brazil and conducted mapping research. Readers will find themselves laughing and thoroughly amazed at the many predicaments the Edwardses encountered while they fulfilled this exciting and vital ministry.

Along the way this husband and wife endured such challenges as—

- trying to learn a language in a foreign culture;
- trying to purchase a bus ticket before they mastered a new language;
- driving 12 different automobiles in one year;
- spending all night on a bus with their seats next to the toilet;
- coping when their vehicle is broken down in an isolated desert area in a foreign country;
- trying to become un-stuck in sand on a beach with the ocean tide fast approaching;
- navigating without a working GPS while in the backwoods of Brazil with darkness about to fall;
- depending totally on strangers for their very survival.

Readers will discover what real missionary life is like as they travel with Paula and Van through these laugh-a-minute yet awe-inspiring misadventures in Northeast Brazil, in which these missionaries constantly experienced God's provision. I trust that God will use what you are about to read to enable you always to seek to follow the life's True Road Map, which is the Word of God.

Wade Akins
IMB Evangelist and Global Church Planting Trainer
Former missionary to Brazil
Author, *Be a 24/7 Christian*

Foreword #2

When I first heard that an "older", short-term missionary couple would be arriving Brazil to do research in some highly remote areas, I thought the idea was crazy. First off, short-term missionaries receive only about three months of language study. Secondly, language learning increases in difficulty in proportion to age. I know this because I celebrated my 50th birthday during language school; I struggled even though I had an entire year of language training. I wasn't sure anyone could survive this assignment with only three months of preparation, but Van and Paula Edwards did.

Leadership asked me to determine a list of "stuff" they would need. A 4x4 vehicle, GPS, wench, tools, repair parts, survival kit, satellite phone, an "OnStar" navigation system, a translator, and a guardian angel all sprang to mind. And that was just to get them from one place to another. I also had to consider housing and furnishings for them as they moved up the coast. This was the first time I had attempted to fill such an order. Between the time the Van and Paula arrived in Brazil and departed for their field, we sustained some budget cuts, so my wish-list went out the window. I know that God is the God of impossible things, but I wondered whether this might be pushing it a bit. God, as always, proved Himself faithful.

Van and Paula limped along in the vehicles that I provided for them and completed their mission successfully. They always were ready and excited to tell of their latest adventure—and they had plenty! I don't recall one time that they lost their sense of the call. They are examples to those who are arriving or have arrived at retirement age. They could have stayed within their comfort zone. They could have stayed close to their adult children and grandkids, but they chose to be obedient to the call on God on their lives.

Read how God protects and provides for His own, but be warned: God may be calling you to leave your comfort zone. In fact, if while you are reading this book the thought occurs to you, *Man, that would be great to do.* or *If I were only (fill in the blank), I would do that,* God is calling you. *And without faith it is impossible to please God* (Heb. 11:6).

May God bless your journey of faith.

Ed Royals, Administrative Associate for Brazil
International Mission Board, SBC

Chapter 1

The Beginning

Everything started innocently enough. One evening we were sitting in our living room doing the usual things. The TV was on, I had a magazine of some type; my husband, Van, was browsing on his laptop. I had no idea what he was studying on his computer, although I was reasonably certain it was something harmless. *Wrong assumption.*

All of a sudden Van called out, "Found us a job."

That was interesting to me, because I didn't know we were looking for one. Anyway, what he said got my attention. To learn more I leaned toward his chair. Turns out he was browsing the site of the International Mission Board of the Southern Baptist Convention; he was surveying opportunities to serve overseas.

At the time Van was the pastor of a small Baptist church in North Central Arkansas. We had been at this church for about three years. In some ways our time there had been good, but we also had experienced many challenges. Recently we had talked about believing that our usefulness at this church had reached an end and that God seemed to be calling us elsewhere. The way God speaks to His children is amazing. We both heard Him; we both heard the same thing—which brings me back to Van's announcement.

"What?" I asked

"I said I found us a job."

"Oh, yeah? Where?"

"Brazil."

"Brazil? Doing what?"

"Mapping."

"Mapping? What does that mean?"

Van can be maddeningly persistent in making me drag everything out of him without offering any unnecessary information that I don't specifically ask for.

"For Pete's sake, tell me!"

"It says 'mapping team needed to explore fishing villages in northeastern Brazil'."

My heart went *thump-thump*. I figured he could hear it, but I wasn't ready to reveal the excitement those simple words caused in me.

"*Hmm*. That could be interesting."

We spent a few minutes discussing the possibility; then I picked up my magazine and pretended to become absorbed in an article while at the same time I watched *Law and Order*. Actually my mind was spinning. I can be maddeningly persistent in hiding my true feelings . . . for a while anyway.

The next day while I was at my job as a band director/music teacher, I had the opportunity to check out the job for myself. I had a study hall that had only one student in it. Our relationship was more one of friendship than teacher-student. I read the job description and then turned and looked at her.

"I'm going to Brazil," I stated bluntly.

She gave me a confused look, so I told her about what had happened the night before and read the job description from the computer in front of me. A slow smile spread across her face. She said, "You're going to Brazil."

I really believed this was going to happen, but at the same time I couldn't imagine going back overseas. I have two grown daughters whom I love fiercely; at the time I had two small grandchildren. How could I leave them for two years? How could I miss out on everything that would be going on? On the other hand, I knew God was speaking to me. If you have ever been in that position, then you understand that when He calls you to a job, you never will be happy doing anything else. If you never have been in that position, you won't understand the way I was feeling at that moment. Believe me, the call is unmistakable.

For two weeks I wrestled with the idea, even though I knew what the final decision would be. I knew I would go to Brazil, but convincing myself actually to admit it out loud in words was difficult. Finally one Sunday after church Van and I went out to eat. Van had mentioned the job in Brazil a couple of times, but he hadn't pressed the issue. He was absolutely ready to go. Now. This minute. But, you see, when a couple accepts a call to missions, it has to be a joint acceptance. If both parties aren't completely on board with the idea, then some sort of compromise has to be reached. This decision is best not forced on anyone. So Van hadn't pressed, but I knew exactly where he stood. The time had arrived for me to let him in on the fact that I was right there beside him. For a long time we sat in the restaurant and talked. I cried. I was so torn. I knew what God wanted me to do. And I wanted to do it, too, but I still had that nagging desire to stay near my family. After spending the biggest part of a year serving in Guatemala in a previous short-term missions assignment, I knew how difficult the separation would be. Ultimately, though, I knew I couldn't put my family and my desires ahead of God's will for my life. So we left the restaurant knowing we would pursue employment with the International Mission Board.

To be accepted for service with the IMB requires an exacting process, but we were hoping the fact that we had served before would hasten the schedule. It must have, because we went home that Sunday night and emailed the IMB, which meant that on Monday the agency received our communication. On Tuesday we had a response. We could begin the procedure to fill the mapping-team position. We were ecstatic.

17

Having finally crossed that line to submit to God, I now was eager to get things on the road. All of this happened in February, but we had lots of things to do before we actually could go to Brazil.

The first item on our list was to resign from our present jobs. I was teaching, so I finished the school year. At the end of May Van resigned his post. In June we sold our house and most of our possessions and moved across the state to Fort Smith to be closer to our daughters while we made preparations to go to Brazil.

Another thing we had to do was to go to Richmond, VA, for training. While there we talked to our advisor. We learned that we could go to Brazil either for two years or three years. We chose to extend our term to three years. In the back of our minds we were thinking we eventually would spend even more time than that in Brazil. We also learned about the requirements to get a visa to Brazil. This sounded as though it was a very straightforward procedure, but from conversations with missionary colleagues in Brazil we knew that getting a visa for that country would be tougher than for Guatemala. The process turned out to be much tougher. Van, the planner and detail person in our unit, began gathering all the things we would need such as his diploma from seminary, his ordination certificate, and birth certificates and our marriage license. Once he was satisfied everything was ready, he sent it to the mission office in Richmond. The mission office promptly wrote back and said the birth certificates and marriage license we had submitted would not be acceptable at the Brazilian consulate. We needed certified copies of our birth certificates and our marriage license. Both of these things had burned in a house fire. So, even though we had the certified copies we had gotten for Guatemala, we would have to get new ones for Brazil from the agencies in the states in which they had been issued: Louisiana and New Mexico. When we checked online about having them sent to us, we discovered that just going to get them would be about as inexpensive and much quicker, but that required a road trip to those two states. We combined business with pleasure by visiting with family in Louisiana and then made the long trek to New Mexico to get my birth certificate. At last we believed we had everything we needed. All that remained was to go to the consulate in Houston and present everything to Brazilian officials there. Two days were necessary to get in to see the consul. When we finally sat down with him, he sat on one side of the glass and we sat on the other as he flipped through the huge pile of documents in front of him. He arrived at my birth certificate—the one we had traveled all the way to New Mexico to get.

"Who's this?" he asked.

"Me," I replied.

"I don't need this," he sneered as he tossed it back to us through the slot at the bottom of the window.

We were flabbergasted. They had specifically asked for originals of our birth certificates.

"But, you asked for it!" Van exclaimed. "We went to New Mexico to get it!"

"No, we never ask for that. It is not in our policy," he asserted.

"But . . .," Van began; then, thinking better of the matter, he let it drop.

After checking through the rest of the papers, the consul told us we could return the next day to get the visas.

We were so relieved! The process had been long and tedious; at last it was over.

We were so excited as we arrived early for our appointment the next day. In just a matter of minutes we would have the visas in our hands and we would be on our way.

The consul entered. We sat together on a love seat; he took a chair near us. Although his attitude seemed a little lighter

19

than it had the day before, he still was a pretty sour person. He began to speak, but we were surprised that he didn't talk about us; he talked about his job and what a thankless position he held. He complained about his co-workers and his work environment. He was a miserable little man. I felt sorry for him. Then he shifted the subject to our visas. That was more like it. I was squirming in my seat.

"Your visas have been approved. You may return to this office next Friday and pick them up."

My sympathy evaporated. Sometimes I am too impulsive; I opened my mouth to argue with him, but Van beat me to the punch.

"Next Friday will be fine. Do we both need to be here, or can I pick them up?"

My jaw dropped as I gaped at my husband. Then I realized the wisdom of his words. Even though this would require another trip from Arkansas to Houston, the process would be over. If we argued, who knew what additional hoops they could find for us to jump through?

The miserable man did his best attempt at a smile.

"You may come alone. We will see you next week."

The next week we *did* get the visas. We were only a month behind our expected departure date. That was not bad.

On January 21, 2007, we boarded the plane for Brazil. It was a trip into the unknown—the first of many adventures . . . although the word *misadventures* ultimately would describe much of what lay before us.

Chapter 2

Getting There

We flew to the city of São Paulo. The trip is a long, grueling overnight flight, so when we arrived the next day, we were pretty well wiped out. On arriving in a country we never had visited before, we had a lot of apprehension. Knowing that we planned to spend the next three years there added to the stress.

The director of the language school, David, and his wife, Ramona, were there to meet us. I never had seen Ramona, but she was able to pick me out of the arriving passengers. At first I thought this happened because of the bewildered, lost look on my face; later I realized our gigantic pile of luggage with our names plastered all over it probably gave her a hint. At any rate, as I passed, she called my name. We piled everything into the Volkswagen van they were driving and made the two-hour drive to Campinas. The mission had a house in which we were to live; it had been stocked with a small amount of basic items. David and Ramona showed us around the house. Then they gave us some necessary instructions and left. For the first time we were on our own. The main thing we wanted to do was to take a long, hot shower and collapse into bed for a while. We would worry about tomorrow . . . tomorrow.

The next day we met Rick and Jill and their daughter, Miranda. They would be our host family while we were in Campinas. Being a host family doesn't require as much as it sounds as though it would. We wouldn't be living in the same house with our host family; this family simply had been given the task of supplying us with basic things to get started in the house and showing us around the town a little to ease our adjustment to Brazilian living. Rick and Jill earlier had served a two-year term in Brazil; now they had returned as career missionaries. They would become great friends.

Our first task was to begin learning the language. *Whoopee!* Actually, I like the challenge of studying another language, but that is not the case for my husband. For him learning a new language is a necessary evil. "Short-term" missionaries such as we were normally go to language school for about three months. Since we had extended our term, we were blessed to get nearly a year of language training. David realized that our assignment was different from that of the usual jobs short-termers have. He knew that once we left the cocoon of language school, we would be on our own without the resource of having career missionaries nearby to help us with the language. We would be sort of like sheep among wolves. We later would learn just how right he was.

During our first few weeks in Brazil, in classes with Priscilla and Vivianne we spent time learning some of the basics of the language and culture. We also scuttled around town getting necessary documents, setting up a bank account, and registering with the federal police. Then we enrolled in Interclass, a private language school in Campinas. At Interclass we met Pierre, Marina, Antonio, Vera, and some of the other teachers. These Brazilian teachers guided us through our struggles with the language. They patiently led us from being total non-speakers to being people who could at least function on our own. They not only were good teachers, they were great people who became good friends. My teacher, Vera, constantly encouraged me to write a book about the experiences we would have doing the mapping job. I could go on and on about our experiences at Interclass, but that would be another book.

Our year in Campinas was wonderful. Without the help of David, Ramona, Priscila, and Vivianne, our experience at the consulate in Houston would have seemed like a walk in the park. We praise God for these wonderful people.

Finally the time had arrived to do what we had traveled here to do. We got ready to move to Salvador, Bahia, and to get to work. The scope of our mapping research was to explore the coastal area up to 10 kilometers inland from the southern border of Bahia all the way to the western border of Maranhão. The distance between those two points is a long way. We had a lot to do.

Going to Salvador meant moving again. I have moved so many times that I'm good at it, but I still don't like it. Moving this time wasn't as difficult as the last time had been, though. All of our things pretty much were gathered together, but I was astounded at how much stuff people can accumulate in just one year. We had an aquarium that I had enjoyed, but now I passed it on to colleagues who had children. I introduced them to the joy of fish. We boxed up and labeled everything else and shipped it ahead of us to Salvador to the missionary house in which we would live. When all of those arrangements were complete, Priscila took us out to the airport. Our bags were packed. We were ready to go. We were leaving on a jet plane.

Chapter 3

Stranded in Bahia

We had been in Salvador for almost three weeks. We were very ready to get to work, but we couldn't do so because we had not received the necessary extensions on our visas. Without the extensions we could not travel legally.

When we left Campinas, we had been told that getting the extensions would not be a problem. Indeed, another missionary family that had left Campinas just before we did already had gotten extensions. When we landed in Salvador, we had been told that all we had to do was to go to the office of federal police. That office was situated in the airport. The people there would take our passports, add the new stamps, and send us on our way. Of course, things weren't that simple for us. When we handed the official our passports, he gave us one of *those looks*. I don't think he understood what we wanted; I know he didn't understand our Portuguese. We did our best, but our best was not good enough. That day we left the airport without our new visas; after all these weeks, we still were trying to get them.

Since the big problem in dealing with the federal police seemed to be the language, we enlisted the help of a missionary friend who spoke excellent Portuguese. We thought she could resolve the issue. We interrupted her schedule and dragged her across town in the crazy Salvadoran traffic to the airport. We were apologetic to her but were confident that she would get us past the barrier to our new visas. Nancy told the man at the counter what we wanted. For some reason he could not give it to us; even Nancy didn't understand the problem.

We were so disappointed. This experience turned out to be just the beginning; in the future we would be making many futile trips to the federal police. Ghosts of visas past loomed in our minds. We had to go back so many times that we quit bothering Nancy and just limped along in our lame Portuguese. Each visit to the federal police was an exercise in frustration. We would think we had everything we needed and brace ourselves for the trip. When we got to the airport, we would explain as much as possible. Then we would give our documents to the young man behind the counter. He would take the papers and look at them studiously. Then he would disappear through a door to consult with his superior, because he didn't have a clue what to do with our documents. Then he and the superior would return to the door so the boss could get a look at us. After that, one or the other of them would explain the next step, whatever it was this time; we would go off on a scavenger hunt trying to satisfy that requirement.

I don't remember how many hoops we jumped through, but at long last we got a real answer. That day we were told that all we had to do was pay the fees and go to a site online on which our names would be listed. When we found our names on the list, we would print them off, take the printout to the office, and the officials would grant our extensions. Simple. We were ecstatic! We believed we had achieved a major milestone. I had to hang on to Van to keep him from doing cartwheels through the airport on our way out. Once we got home, he sat down at the computer and found the list they had told us about. Yes, we were right there on the list. Seeing this kind of warmed my heart. We were so close. The next day we were eager to go back to the airport. Our truck knew the way, so all we had to do was ride. After all this time we finally were getting results.

With big smiles we proudly presented to the man our documents and our receipt for payment of the fees. He didn't smile. He just looked at the printout and then calmly pointed out to us that the date was wrong. We stared at him and then at the document in his hand. After a bit we realized that they had printed the wrong year.

"Well, the publisher made a typo. No big deal," we said. "You can just change it or make a note of the error and give us the necessary documents."

The man gave us a pitying look. *Poor Americans*, his look seemed to say. Then he slowly shook his head.

We were astounded. I mean, after all, the mistake was theirs. Back home something like this would have been noted, officially changed then and there, and we would be happily on our way. We were jerked back to the reality that we weren't "back home" when he told us we would have to wait until the mistake had been corrected and published again. With a sad smile he passed the paper back across to us. We left almost in tears.

We knew that we weren't in Brazil to play solitaire on the computer. We had a job to do. We had a great four-wheel-drive vehicle of which we were very proud; it was just itching to hit the road. In our frustration we called the mission office in Brasilia to find out whether we could travel without our visa extensions. Thankfully we got permission to go as long as we stayed in Bahia.

In Brazil, Carnaval, the world's largest party, is a crazy time. The celebration is crazier in some areas of the country than others, though; Salvador happens to be one of the craziest areas. Besides having parties and partiers in all parts and the drunken danger that goes along with that, a good possibility existed that we wouldn't be able to find a place to stay on the road. If we could find a place, we would have to pay inflated vacation prices. After taking all of this into consideration, we decided to venture north of Salvador instead of going way south as we originally had planned. We would be back in Salvador before Carnaval, so we could hide out in the mission house for the duration. At least we could go.

When we set out that February morn on our first trip, we seemed as though we were people freed from prison; we were setting out to do something brand new. The sun was shining, we had a great truck, and we were on the road. Life was good . . . at last.

We were especially happy to have the SUV that had been assigned to us. During language school we had gotten the jalopies from the bottom of the barrel. I think they gave us the worst ones since we were a couple with no children at home. If we got stranded on the road, at least no little ones would be involved. In the year we had been in Campinas, we had driven at least 10 or 12 different cars. Only two of them officially were assigned to us, but whenever our assigned vehicle broke down, we got to experience another one. This SUV was beautiful. I'm not a car connoisseur, but I really appreciated this truck. This truck looked as though it could deal with any situation we would encounter.

Since our job involved small towns and Salvador is a very big one, we traveled a long way to get to the point in which we actually could start working. I was the map reader and navigator; Van did all the driving. After I studied the map, I determined our first "target" would be the town of Conde situated a couple of hours north of Salvador.

Conde was not the type of village we were seeking, but it was a pleasant town. As we drove around, we didn't see a Baptist church. Since Conde was outside the parameters of our work, we continued on to Sitio do Conde situated right on the waterfront. Sitio do Conde was too big, too, but the map showed roads leading away from it in both directions. We decided to find a place to stay. The next morning we would visit the other towns.

Our first experience in overnight lodging was extremely dismal. We spent the night in a dreadful, but cheap, *pousada*. A *pousada* is what people in the United States would consider a motel, but in Brazil a distinct difference exists. *Café da manhã*—breakfast—was included, but it was pretty dreadful, too.

The next morning we took a sand road that led down the coast from Sitio do Conde. We entered the first "fishing village" we had ever seen. The place was amazing. The entrance to the village was lined with straw huts that were home to the people living and working there. *This is why we're here*, we thought as we gaped and stared. As we drove on through town past the Catholic church, we were delighted to see a Baptist church. To see the church was even more astonishing than the town itself was.

We continued to a tiny village in which the road ended at the ocean. We stopped at a little restaurant there and tried out our Portuguese on the very gracious owner. We were able to get some information from him; in return we decided to have a snack at his place. Sitting under the umbrella on the beach, digging our toes into the warm sand, and watching the waves while we waited for him to bring the fried fish out to us was tough, but somehow we endured. That was the best fish I have ever eaten. I don't think I'll ever have any better.

After "brunch" we struck out again—all fortified and ready to take on the world. We went as far as the border between Seregipe and Bahia. The border was our limit, so when we reached it, we turned back. For two novice researchers we had had a successful outing. We were feeling rather smug. To us things in the foreseeable future looked very bright. That's because we had forgotten that no such thing as *the foreseeable future* exists.

On our return trip, we dipped into Conde thinking we would spend the night there again. In the end we were defeated in our search for a suitable place, because we had not yet developed the knack for finding a *pousada*. We didn't want to go back to the place in which we had stayed the previous night. Further south we knew of a "tourist-friendly" city in which we knew we would find a place. Going there seemed as though it was a good idea, so we headed that way. That's when the foreseeable future became the present. We were about 12 kilometers from Conde when Van suddenly said, "We've got a problem."

I'm always amazed at how I can talk to Van for hours and he never hears me, but let the truck say, "*Ow!*", and it's like an alarm. Before he had time to pinpoint the problem—before I ever heard anything—we heard a loud *bang*. The truck quit completely as we coasted to the side of the road. Steam was billowing from in front. We stared at each other. This couldn't be good. The sun was going down; the hour was late. We were on the side of the road nowhere near anything in a country with which we were unfamiliar and in which the people spoke a language we barely understood. The highway stretched out for miles in either direction. From the hilltop we were on we couldn't see a house or even another car. All around the twilight was ominously silent except for the slight sizzle emanating from the wounded engine. We were stunned. *How could our beautiful truck let us down this way?* The situation gave new meaning to the old saying that beauty is only skin-, or in this case paint-, deep. After we considered our options, we arrived at the conclusion that we didn't have any. We were going to have to hoof it.

As we held hands, we crouched behind the car and prayed that God would provide someone to help us. Then we started walking. This walk wasn't the most pleasant walk I had ever taken, but it turned out to be a short one. After only about five minutes three guys in a bob truck stopped across the highway from us. My heart was in my throat. In this case I wanted someone to stop, but I didn't want anyone to stop. *Was this a good thing or a bad thing?* We felt a little bit anxious; we ran across the road and found the answer to our prayer. The driver had realized that the broken-down truck must have been ours and offered to take us back to Conde. The passengers climbed on the back and gave us the seats in the cab. We were so grateful, but our deficiency in the language prevented us from expressing this to the driver. Our limited conversation was peppered with lots of heartfelt smiles.

Now, in the States when someone gives you a ride, that's that. He gets you to somewhere, drops you off, and waves goodbye. He exhibits a "be-warmed-and-well-fed" sort of attitude. Not so in Brazil. Once this driver had picked us up, we became his responsibility sort of like the guy in the story of the Good Samaritan. Mr. Trucker went to a store and asked all sorts of questions about *guinchos* (tow trucks) and *oficinas* (mechanic shops). Praise God he was there to do the asking. We understood only a little of what he was saying, but our vocabulary was enlarging quickly. He learned where a 24-hour towing service was situated and took us there, but, you guessed it, the 24-hour service provider was not in service at this time. Maybe it was the 25th hour.

Obviously thinking that he couldn't just leave us standing around on the street, Mr. Trucker continued to haul us around as he looked for help. Now we were getting concerned about delaying him. About that time a friendly local taxi driver picked up on our dilemma and stepped in to relieve the truck driver. For Sandro, the taxi driver, hauling us around sure beat standing on the corner waiting for a fare to arrive. We gave Mr. Trucker a large tip; he released us into Sandro's capable hands.

After several phone calls Sandro finally made contact with the tow-truck owner. By now the hour was late, but we didn't dare leave the truck out there exposed to thieves all night. Even if the truck couldn't be driven away, many things could be removed from the truck and sold, to say nothing of our things loaded in it. We followed the wrecker back out to the place in which the truck had broken down. In the moonlight, all prim and lovely, sat the SUV! *Such a fake!*

At long last they got the SUV on the wrecker and got the wrecker back to Conde. We were exhausted. We had had a long day topped off with a stressful, emotionally-draining event. Sandro decided that we needed a hotel, so he took us to the nicest place in Sitio do Conde and got us installed for the night. The nicest place in Sitio do Conde actually was a very nice place that was quite unlike the *pousada* of the night before. Sandro knew more about finding one than we did. We made arrangements for Sandro to meet us at the hotel the next morning at eight. You see, we now were his responsibility; he would take care of us until the end of this ordeal. We slept well that night.

We already had learned enough about the Brazilian concept of schedules to know that the Brazilians basically don't have them. Since Sandro was Brazilian, we weren't really expecting to see him until after we had eaten breakfast. *Shame on us!* I guess Sandro had learned enough about Americans to know that when they said to meet at a certain time, they meant *at that time*. Even before we arrived the next morning, Sandro was in the dining room waiting for us. However, he didn't intrude on our breakfast. While we ate, he made himself useful as he watered the hotel's plants.

After breakfast we renewed our search for a place to get the SUV repaired. We also were concerned about how we would get home. We were in a dither. The conversation went something like this:

Van: "How are we going to get the car fixed?"

Paula: "Where will we stay tonight?"

Van: "How can we get back to Salvador?"

Paula: "What are we going to do with our stuff?"

Van: "What do you do with a dead SUV?"

It sounded like that game in which you speak in questions only. Like a tennis fan Sandro watched us back and forth. Finally we both looked at him and, in our best Portuguese, asked, "What are we going to do?"

Although we were rattled, Sandro was calmly relishing this exciting detour from his boring routine.

"No problem," he said. "Let's go talk to the *guincho* driver."

We hopped into his cab and away we went. Mr. Towfellow had checked with the mechanic next door and was told that the SUV indeed was dead. Only the people at a dealership would be able to resurrect it; Sandro thought he might be able to find someone in Conde with the requisite skills. He took us on a back-street tour of Conde and visited all of the shady shade-tree mechanics he knew. No one was willing to even take a look at the truck.

We resumed our "questions-only" game right where we had left off. Our biggest concern was getting us and the SUV back to Salvador. Sandro was driving and listening to us banter back and forth. He didn't understand the language, but he understood the tone. Suddenly without one concern about other traffic he stopped right in the middle of the street in the middle of the square. He turned, looked at us, said, "*Calma!*

Calma! I will take you back to Salvador!" And there you have it. Problem solved. "You Americans worry too much," he said as he shook his head.

We went back to Mr. Towfellow to make arrangements for him to haul the truck back to Salvador. Then we took off heading south. Personally, at this point, I think this whole trip had gone south.

The idea was that we travel with the wrecker, but before we were out of Conde, Sandro sped off and left it way behind. We had passed the place at which we had broken down before Sandro finally pulled to the side of the road to wait. I can't express how happy I was to be sitting on the side of the road in Bahia again. At least we were in daylight and the car in which we rode would move on its own. Finally the tow truck appeared. We fell in behind it and made a merry little caravan to the car dealership in Salvador. It was the longest taxi ride I had ever taken. Of course, that's not saying much, because up until that time, I had been in a taxi only three or four times in my life. Once we got to Salvador, Sandro continued his assumed caretaker duty. With all the practice he had gotten, he was pretty good at understanding our version of Portuguese. He did a great job of translating our problem to the folks at the dealership. We were very grateful to him.

After we made the necessary arrangements to get the truck checked out, Sandro drove us home. By now he was like an old friend. We were kind of sad to see him go. He looked exhausted, so I was glad to see them load his taxi on the wrecker so he wouldn't have to drive home. We gave him a soft drink, paid him, and sent him on his way. Then the gate closed behind him; we were on our own again. Back in Salvador without a vehicle. Back waiting to go to work again.

Although we would not have chosen to break down, it had been a remarkable experience. We had been exposed to a huge

chunk of Brazilian culture and, with God's help, we had sur-
vived. We knew we could tackle the job we had accepted. We
had interacted with the locals; our vocabulary had increased. I
now knew the Portuguese word for *head gasket*!

Chapter 4

The Other Car

After the SUV left us stranded on the side of the road, we found ourselves back in Salvador wondering what we would do now. We surely couldn't do coastal mapping on foot! For the time being we only could wait and see.

Sometimes making your own decisions is a good thing. Sometimes having someone else make them for you is good. This was one of those times in which we were happy to turn this problem over to someone else. We called Ed.

Ed was the man who at that time dealt with all the cars and housing for the mission. I was glad I didn't have his job. He was the person we had called when the SUV had broken down. He knew all about our car problems.

After much discussion, debate, and many phone calls we decided that the SUV would be shipped to Brasilia, where the mission was headquartered, to be repaired properly. While the SUV languished at the dealership and waited to be picked up, we languished at the house itching to do something productive. Besides needing a truck to do our work we needed a vehicle for everyday errands and such.

Unlike our house in Campinas, the house in Salvador was not close to anything except other houses. In Campinas we could walk to some of the places we needed to go; in Salvador we had to drive everywhere. We considered using the truck belonging to the missionary in whose house we were living, but that was nixed. Then we learned that another missionary husband and wife were going to leave the field and go back to the States. Since they were working in Bahia, until further notice they would leave their car at our house. We were sad to see them go but delighted to see their car. Having this car seemed as though it was a good temporary solution to our "no-wheels" situation. This vehicle was a small sedan, not a honking, big, four-wheel drive truck like the SUV, but even this car was certainly better than walking. A car like this would not serve well for the job we would be doing, but at least we could drive around town . . . or so we thought. Van went out to check out our new ride. He did a little cleaning. The car seemed OK, but he did wonder why a big jug of water was in the trunk. The other missionaries had little kids, so maybe they always wanted to have some water for emergency clean-up. *Oh well,* he thought as he set the jug on the porch, *we won't need that.*

Later that day we took our "new" car out for its maiden voyage with us. Our mission was to go to the grocery store to get a few items. That entailed driving down the oceanfront highway about four or five kilometers; we didn't think our little errand would be a big deal. The ocean-front highway, or *orla*, is a long, scenic boulevard. For miles you have a beautiful view of the ocean. However, the fact that the *orla* is a boulevard also means that you often have to go a long way the wrong way before you can get turned around to go the right way. The grocery store was on "our side" of the boulevard, so to arrive home we would have to go several blocks farther down the boulevard to loop back.

We hadn't gone far from home before we realized the car was making a very strange noise unlike any sound I had ever heard a car make. The sound was sort of a *boing* sound. Van said the noise sounded as though someone was trying to tune a kettle drum. He thought the sound was very funny. I didn't. I like my cars to make nice car sounds without being creative. Besides, my recent experience with recalcitrant cars didn't put me in a humorous frame of mind. To add to my discontent we were in the usual heavy Salvadoran traffic. Unless you've experienced Brazilian driving, you can't begin to imagine what the traffic in Salvador is like. I think its traffic is one of the best examples of bad Brazilian driving. I was distinctly uncomfortable being in that crazy mess in a car that was making quite un-carlike sounds. We had to spend quality time sitting in traffic and dodging buses before we even got to the store. Once we got to the store, in short order we picked up our few items. By the time we left, I was thinking that maybe things would be OK after all. As we exited the store, home was to our left. We couldn't go left from the parking lot. We had to go right before we could go left. Normally that would be just a mild inconvenience, but today wasn't normal. Today we were in this car.

Besides hair-raising traffic, another thing on which you always can rely in Salvador is that the weather will be hot. Today was no exception to that rule. Van kicked on the air-conditioner. From the vents hot air rushed into our faces. That was not good. We turned the AC off. He lowered all the windows. Here we were creeping along in thick traffic in a car that made weird sounds and had no air-conditioning. *Fun.*

The beachfront road in Salvador is one of its busiest. With Carnaval just around the corner, the normally heavy traffic was even heavier. Since this was the case, the works department had decided that now would be a good time to get the road in good shape. One lane of traffic had been closed off to fix the holes on that side. Choking the cars down to one lane really gummed up things. While we were stopped in the bottlenecked traffic, the purpose of the water jug became evident.

The car began to overheat. Steam started creeping from under the hood. OK, this situation was not making me happy. I absolutely did not want to break down again. I especially did not want to break down in the middle of the day in the middle

of the Salvadoran traffic with no means of escape. That would
be worse than being out in the middle of nowhere on the side
of the highway. As the traffic crept along, I sweated from
nerves as well as from the heat. Right along with mine the
temperature of the car continued to rise. We passed the turnoff
to our house, but unfortunately we couldn't make the turn
from where we were, because that street was on the other side
of the boulevard. We still had several blocks to go before we
got to the u-turn to return. We discussed the possibility of
jumping the median but decided that would mortally wound
this ailing car. I prayed that we would just be able to get back
home. *So close but so far away!* Finally, after what seemed an
eternity, we made the u-turn into the home stretch. I could
breathe again. I believed we would get home after all. *Thank
you, Lord.* Now that we were going the other way, we could
move along at a good clip. The fast-flowing air cooled the car.
Soon we were home. I vowed I wouldn't go out in that car
again . . . at least not today.

That evening we got a phone call from Ed. He knew that
we needed to get to work but that we didn't have a car. He
also knew that the missionaries who were leaving the country
would be leaving their car in Salvador. He had a suggestion
for us.

"I know this is not the best solution," he began when I
answered the phone, "but some missionaries are going home.
Their car will be in Salvador. Perhaps you could use . . .."

"No, no, and no," I interrupted.

Ed was a little surprised, since I usually leave these decisions to Van, but this was one decision I was going to make
for myself!

Chapter 5

To Recife on a Bus

When Van explained to Ed why we couldn't use the other missionary's car, Ed had to find an alternate plan. Ed had a challenging job. Figuring out a way to get us on the road was only one small part of his duties. I didn't envy Ed, but I did admire him for the good job he did. In only a couple of days we got another call from him.

"OK," he told Van. "Here's the best solution I can find. In Recife we have a truck that is not assigned to anyone right now. The truck is a small, four-door pickup with four-wheel drive. I think the thing is running good. Of course, the obvious problem is that this truck is in Recife; Recife is more that 800 kilometers from you."

Van nodded his head. He was giving me the gist of the conversation.

"How are you going to get the truck here?" he asked.

"Well, that's the catch. *I'm* not going to get the pickup. *You* are."

"*Uh-huh*. I see. How am I going to do that?" Van asked. He dreaded the answer.

"Well," Ed hemmed and hawed. "Uh, you can take a bus."

"A bus . . . OK. *Uh-huh*. I see," he repeated. "How do I do that?"

"That's easy. Just go to the bus station, find this company, and buy a ticket. I'm sure Danny will help you."

Van paused a long time while he considered this new information. I knew that dancing in his head were visions of the federal police and acquiring a visa.

Getting our visa extension wasn't supposed to be difficult either. After a bit he spoke into the phone.

"Well, OK," he sighed. "We'll see what we can do."

"Good deal. Good deal," Ed said. He clearly was pleased with Van's response. I could hear the relief in his voice. I imagined him doing a little jig. "The buses in Brazil are good. Some of them even have beds in them. They are comfortable."

Ed was driving home his sale, but he didn't have to. We realized that, once again, we didn't have lots of choices. We could go to Recife on a bus and get a truck, or we could stagnate in the house in Salvador. Going to Recife didn't look too bad. The trip would be another adventure.

After Van hung up the phone, we discussed how we were going to pull this off. We never had done this sort of thing before, but we were learning that we could be highly resourceful when we had to be. I mean, surely buying a bus ticket couldn't be tougher than getting the air-conditioner in the SUV repaired. We had done that. Buying this ticket would be easier than talking to the wrecker driver, the people at the car dealership, and the federal police. We had managed that. However, we did see one small problem. We didn't even know where the bus station was. We took Ed's suggestion; we called Danny, our friend in Salvador. He told us where to find the station. He said he could meet us later. That sounded as though it was a plan, so we talked the guard at the gate into calling a cab for us. Then we went on down to the station.

For a while we waited for Danny, but apparently he had gotten delayed. We were eager to get started, so we decided to attempt to make the purchase on our own. Van called Danny. He told him our new plan. If we had problems, we would let him know. Buying a bus ticket turned out to be nothing like our visit to the federal police. In fact, making the purchase wasn't as trying as air-conditioner repair. The endeavor was very simple. In no time at all we were booked for a road trip to Recife. We were going to get more cultural experience and see more of the country.

The bus left Salvador about 8 p.m. Getting to Recife would take all night, but when we got to Recife, we would be staying with colleagues. All we had to do was get to Recife.

The bus was comfortable, but we discovered very quickly that we had chosen poorly when we selected our seats. Our choice was right across from the restroom. We had learned another lesson. We traveled through the night. The bus stopped several times. We had numerous interruptions by folks going to the bathroom. I, who can sleep just about anywhere, slept a lot. Unfortunately, Van didn't. I remember waking up from time to time and looking out the window. All I ever saw were the hills that lined the road. To me the whole trip seemed as if we were going through a long tunnel.

Early in the morning we got to the bus station in Recife. I looked as though I had slept in my clothes; Van looked as though he hadn't slept at all. The station was huge and busy—more like an airport than a bus station. I think Americans could learn something about bus travel from the Brazilians. The trip had not been bad. The bus seats definitely were more comfortable than coach-class airplane seats. Travel by bus in Brazil is efficient and reasonably priced. Letting someone else do the driving suited me, too.

We wandered around vaguely looking for our friend, Brent, but diligently looking for coffee. Coffee definitely was our first priority. We had just sat down with our coffee when Brent rushed through the doors looking like a man going to a fire. He greeted us heartily, but when we indicated we were not finished with our coffee, he began fairly dancing around. He had a meeting; we needed to leave right now! I took a last sip of my coffee before I followed the two men out to the waiting truck. Brent drove as though he still hadn't found that fire! I kept glancing nervously at the speedometer; I thought we were going to get a ticket. However, I could do nothing except hang on and pray. We arrived at Brent's house without incident.

While we were in Recife, we were looking forward to visiting with Rick and Jill, the friends we had known longest in Brazil. I mean, golly, we had known them a year or so. Next door to Brent's house was an empty missionary house, but we wanted to stay in a hotel. The empty mission house was really, well, empty. Rick suggested we go ahead and find a hotel. He was familiar with Recife, he said, so he was going to be the navigator. He ensconced himself in the shotgun seat. Jill and I got in the back with Miranda. Then we were off on our hotel-hunting expedition.

Rick had a map, but he had a difficult time reading the street signs and the map at the same time. He would find the street on the map just as he saw the street on the ground.

"Turn here," he would say at the last possible minute. "Now go up that street."

"Here?" Van would ask as he was turning.

"No! No! That street!" Rick would point.

The fact that Van was working on almost no sleep didn't make driving easier for him. The traffic here made me think of another city with which I was familiar. The streets were filled with cars, buses, and trucks. In one area a bunch of buses were clogging up the street. We got to sit behind them for a while, but we didn't find what we were looking for: hotels. Looking for lodging we went up one street and down another. Again I had to admire Van's driving skill. I was thankful he was driving instead of me.

All of a sudden Rick pointed across the viaduct. "We need to be across the way!" he exclaimed.

When Van whipped into the next street, he accidentally

crossed a viaduct going the wrong way! Thinking quickly he swooped into the first side street he saw. Later on in the mail we got a picture of that turn along with a ticket for turning like that. Even though all of us were safely buckled in, the police, just for fun, threw in a ticket for not wearing a seat belt.

By now Van was tired and frazzled. We were no closer to finding a hotel than when we had begun. We decided to scrap the whole hotel idea and stay in the sparsely furnished mission house after all. In the end we had a better time visiting with our friends at that house than we would have at a hotel any way.

After breakfast the next morning we said goodbye and then started south toward Salvador. We had a long trip ahead of us, but we were happy to be working. We prayed that we would arrive back in Salvador without problems. Actually, we kind of believed we had had our share of problems recently. Our "new" truck seemed to be running well. I already knew this little vehicle could go fast. Right now, though, we weren't interested in speed. We were interested in getting out of Recife. I brought out the map book we had bought in Campinas. Before long we were on a delightful road known as Brazil 101—a highway straight out of some Stephen King-esque horror novel. The traffic was deadly; I was not a happy camper at all. However, once we were out of the city, things got better. To me, things always seem to get better when we get out of the city . . . whatever the city might be.

Our first stop after leaving Recife was Porto de Galinhos. Literally, that is Port of the Chickens. Somewhere I read why the town was called by that name, but I don't remember now. I think the port originally was a shipping port and a fishing village, but the village has grown way beyond that today. The town is a beautiful place to visit—full of tourist attractions. I don't remember seeing any chickens at all.

We spent the night at the nearby town of Sirinhaém. This was our first time to stay in a *pousada* since our ill-fated visit to northern Bahia and Conde. We were in the area during the off-season. That was a good thing and a bad thing. That was good because the hotels and *pousada*s would be likely to have vacancies; prices probably would be cheaper. That was bad, because some of the places were closed for the season; finding a place to stay would be more difficult. Still being rookies at the job at this point, we waited until too late to start looking. We asked around the town about lodgings. Finally we got directions to a *pousada*. The man told us to go down a certain road until we passed the 32nd *lombada* (speed bump) The *pousada* would be on the left. We found the place, but the hotel appeared to be closed. We knocked on the gate anyway. Before long a man answered our knock. When we explained that we needed a place to stay for one night, he seemed surprised. Apparently people usually stayed longer than that, but he priced a room to us. We took the room.

The room turned out to be a very nice suite. The *pousada* was very quiet and private, since we were the only people at the inn at the time. Taking advantage of the pool, we had a nice evening swim. That is something we rarely do, since Van doesn't like to swim. The next morning we were able to appreciate the beautifully landscaped grounds that were surrounded by a tall wall. The domestic rabbits that were running freely about were friendly. At this *pousada* I saw my first cashew on the tree.

Our original plan to tackle this job was to go to the southern border of Bahia and work northward. That idea had been torpedoed by the breakdown of the SUV. Since we had had to go to Recife, we developed an alternate plan. Our new plan was to work our way back to Salvador. With that in mind we left Highway 101 (not that that bothered me). Then we traveled south on roads as close to the oceanfront as possible. By following these roads we would sometimes find ourselves on high bluffs near the ocean but above the water. We went many kilometers on crude dirt roads without passing any significant population, let alone actual towns. As we went farther south, we began to find lots of tourist destinations but no fishing villages of the type for which we were searching. Apparently, at least in this part of the country, the fishermen had been sucked into the tourist community. Brazil seemed to be finding a more lucrative way to use its oceans and beaches. We saw fishermen, but they were living all mixed in with everyone else in larger towns. Happily, in most of the larger towns we also found Baptist churches.

Since we always took the road less-traveled, we sometimes saw wonderful, wild beaches that the tourists hadn't discovered yet. At other times, the road would wind away from the beach. Following these types of roads is how we managed to wander into Barra de Santo Antônio through the back door. We were really surprised to find a Baptist church in the town. The pastor, his wife, and two helpers were working at the church. For a few minutes we talked to them. They told us about several more towns between Santo Antônio and Maceió that had Baptist churches. That made us happy.

When we were ready to leave, they told us that the easiest route south would be to take the *balsa* (ferry boat) across the inlet. From the opposite side of the inlet we could continue along the coast to Maceió. This was our first experience in using a *balsa*. It was the first time Van had ever been on a ferry. At the time we didn't know that *balsa*s were going to be a big part of our travel.

Ferries in Brazil can be big, modern vessels with several levels that can carry many cars, or they can be simple boats that move one or two cars at a time. The one in Barra de Santo

Antônio fell into the middle category. This ferry wasn't huge, but the boat was large enough to haul several cars. We felt comfortable driving aboard. Actually the trip turned out to be quite fun.

That day we went as far as the city of Maceió. We decided to spend the night at Praia do Francês just south of Maceió. The trip from Recife to Salvador is a long one. Even though we had covered the area to Maceió quickly because of all the tourist development, we were tired. We needed a while to recharge. The next morning we started toward home to rest for a few days.

Chapter 6

Pacatuba . . . and Pack
Your Sleeping Bag, Too

After a few days at "home" regrouping and taking care of
a few tasks, we backtracked to Maceió to work in the area
between that city and Salvador. As with all the large cities
along the coast, Maceió has spread its influence for a long way
in either direction. We saw many lovely beaches covered with
beachgoers, but if any of them was fishing, he or she was
stirred in with the mix.

About 40 kilometers south of the Maceió metropolitan area
we arrived at Lagoa Azeda. This little settlement was just the
kind of fishing village we had been expecting to see. The little
hamlet was in a beautiful setting. The main street ran right
along the ocean. That day the sky had not one cloud. The
aquamarine-colored ocean sparkled. Bobbing in the surf were
many *jangadas*, the typical, traditional fishing boats Brazilians
use. Some off-duty fishermen were drinking and visiting at the
obligatory bar/restaurant. We eased down the street and took in
the sights and took photos until the street ended. Then we
stopped, got out, and talked to a young man we saw. He
wasn't very forthcoming, but we did learn a little. One thing
he told us was that a town about 30 kilometers away had a
Baptist church. To an American's way of thinking, 30 kilometers (about 18 miles) doesn't seem far. However, when you
consider that most of the folks in Lagoa Azeda don't have a
car, the distance becomes a long, long way to attend church.

As we headed back to the car, I noticed a young woman
passing by; she appeared to have a Bible in her hand.
Emboldened, I approached her and asked her about the Bible.

She told me she had been to a Bible study with an Assembly of God group. I told her what we were about. We quickly realized that we were sisters in Christ. I was happy to learn that the town had some evangelical work. From the truck I grabbed a bunch of tracts to give her so she could share with others. As we left the town behind, we felt encouraged but committed to trying to get Baptist missionaries to work in this village, too.

Continuing down the coast we encountered several towns that had no Baptist churches. When we stopped to eat lunch, the server was eager to talk to us about our work. She was an active member of the Assemblies group in Coruripe. She told us the town had a Baptist church, too.

That night we stayed at a *pousada* right on the beach. The night was beautiful. The view from our window of a full moon reflected in the ocean was splendid. Like glitter its light sparkled across the waves. The surf crashed on the beach just yards below us. For a long time I sat and gazed at the moon. I am convinced that no one puts on a light show like God does.

Unfortunately for Van, the mosquito magnet, the room did have a few extra guests . . . mosquitoes. He got eaten up by them. I didn't have one bite. Is tasting good a good thing or a bad thing? Personally, I think having good taste is better.

The next morning we hit the road early. We reached the conclusion that the beaches in the overlooked state of Alagoas in which we worked were among Brazil's best-kept secrets. One locale in particular, Pontal do Peba, was spectacular.

We drove down the beach and saw a wide variety of activity. This place was a true fishing village but not a small one. We saw men with horse carts driving into the edge of the water to collect the morning's catch from the boats. Other men were working on the hulls of a long row of boats that were beached during low tide. We weren't the only strangers in town. A bunch of tourists crowded into a Range Rover that was emblazoned with some sort of logo. They had their cameras out to get the best shots possible of everything going on. I snapped a good picture of the people taking pictures. Besides seeing the fishermen we saw nice hotels and people catering to the kite-surfing crowd. Of course we saw the usual skimpily-dressed beachgoers enjoying the water and the sun. Because the beach curved here, we could see for miles along the coast. Leaving the beach we drove down a cobblestoned street. Then we wended our way back to the highway.

Our travel that day took us to the border between Alagoas and Seregipe. After the stunning beauty of Pontal do Peba, we had turned inland. We crossed countryside that was pretty bleak. We had learned that a city near Pontal do Peba had a Baptist church, but after that we saw very few churches of any kind.

As the day drew to a close, we began to look for a place to stay. On a *balsa* we crossed the São Francisco River, the second-largest river in Brazil. Then we were in the State of Seregipe. We were becoming old hands with this *balsa* thing.

Our first impression of Seregipe was not very good. First we had gone only a little way toward the coast when the road became a dirt road. We blundered along until we found the coastal town in which we had planned to spend the night. The town was awful; its streets were crowded with people who glared at us as we passed. That was the first time we had been in a place in which we felt a little afraid. I didn't like that feeling.

"Let's get out of here," I told Van. "This place gives me the creeps."

"I agree," he said, "but where will we spend the night? Do you see another place on the map that looks promising?"

"Not really. The best place seems to be Pacatuba."

"OK. We'll try that."

Here we were, once again, searching for a place to pass the night that now was quickly approaching. We started looking for Pacatuba.

I couldn't help but smile at the name. As a musician I pictured a man packing a tuba around on his back just looking for a place to perform. We found this "tuba" without problems, but the town was less than encouraging. This town looked more as though it was a sousaphone than a tuba. As we wandered around, we saw only one sign that indicated a *pousada*. We saw the sign, but we didn't see the *pousada*.

By nature I'm very shy about approaching strangers on the street, but I was learning to get over that. We stopped in the square in front of the place with the sign. I hopped out and went over to the women sitting on the sidewalk in front of the little restaurant under the sign.

"*Boa tarde!* (Good afternoon)," I said in my best Portuguese as I smiled.

They smiled back. That always was a good sign. After our afternoon tour in the nearby town the smiles looked particularly welcoming.

"We're looking for the *pousada*," I said as I indicated the sign. "Can you tell me where to go?"

"The *pousada* is right here," one woman responded.

I glanced around, but I didn't see a *pousada*.

"We have rooms," the woman continued, "but we don't have any vacancies right now."

I sighed.

"The lady next door sometimes has rooms to rent, too. I'll go see if she has one," she said as she rose and ducked through a doorway tucked in between her place and the one next door.

When she returned a few minutes later, she said that the woman did have a room.

What a relief! We met with the neighbor. She led us up a twisting stairway and past a little sitting room down to the far end of the hallway. I never did figure out why we always were given the room the longest distance from the front door.

She explained that her place was more like a rooming house than a *pousada*. She told us that guests were asleep in the front rooms. The room she showed us was small. The bed sagged in the middle. The attached bathroom was like a tiny closet containing a cold shower and a commode. We told her we would stay.

"Would you like sheets and towels?" she asked as she was leaving.

We stared at each other. I knew Van was thinking, "Well, yeah. Sheets and towels would be a real plus," but we simply nodded at her.

"OK," she replied, "but I have to iron the sheets first." She smiled at us again as she left the room.

We went to the truck to get our stuff. As we passed the women at the restaurant, we asked them where we could park.

"Oh, you can just leave your car in the square," one of the women said.

I saw Van's shoulders droop. That was against the rules. On several occasions we had been severely warned not to park on the street. Our car would be gone or stripped when we got back, we were told.

"Are you sure? Will it be safe?" he asked them. "I don't know about this," he muttered to me. "I just don't like it."

But the women assured us the pickup would be safe. After all, our truck was the only vehicle in the square.

With a shrug that signaled his resignation to the inevitable, Van set out for the truck to gather our valuables. We lugged everything worth anything up that long flight of stairs and down the hallway. We did our best to tiptoe past the rooms in which the sleeping people were.

Before long the proprietress reappeared with the ironed sheets. They looked so good and smelled nice, too. Those sheets represented one of the brightest spots in what had turned into a dreary day.

For a while we visited with the proprietress. She told us that her husband was confined to a wheelchair after a motorcycle struck him several years earlier. The accident also had caused brain damage. She supported them by renting out rooms in her house.

After we chatted for a while, we asked her about a place to eat. She considered for a moment. Then she concluded that Juca's place next door was about the best choice. Since the place was highly recommended (and we just didn't want to look for another place), we ventured over. Juca and his wife prepared a delicious, traditional, authentic, Brazilian supper for us. We were famished. The meal was delicious.

Along with supper Juca served up some homespun hospitality. He shared the fact that he had been Mormon, but now, if anything, he was maybe a spiritist. That concerned us. We witnessed to him as much as we could. We also left our cards and some tracts with him. He did tell us that some of his friends were Baptist. He said Pacatuba had a Baptist church.

We slept well on the saggy bed in the hole-in-the-wall *pousada*. The next morning we had breakfast with Juca. The meal was another feast and another fun time. Then Juca sent us on our way with a jar of his homegrown honey. We knew we never would forget our night in Pacatuba.

From Pacatuba we followed dirt roads that snaked through an area of small farms. We were on bluffs high above sea level, but far below in the distance we could see the ocean. We didn't see any fishing villages way up where we were. We looked for Baptist churches, but churches of any kind were rare.

The population was scattered along these roads. Real towns were few and far between. The towns we did pass through were poor. None of the roads was paved. This was the bleakest landscape I had seen in Brazil up until that time. When we finally left that part behind, I was really happy.

When we crossed the border into Bahia, we found the community of Costa Azul. This tiny little settlement had only about 100 houses. We saw a restaurant, so we stopped to talk.

The people had a small parrot as a pet. He appealed to the animal-lover in me. I enjoyed watching him. We talked briefly with the owner before we ordered fried fish for lunch. The fish was delicious, but the flies were so thick we had to continually wave our hands over the food to keep from having the flies as garnishes. Antonio, the owner, saw our plight. With a dish towel in hand he walked over to help us shoo flies. After we finished eating, Van struck up a conversation with Antonio. Antonio told Van that Costa Azul had no church. He pleaded with him to bring one to the community. Van was very moved by such a request. He promised to do what he could.

Although we didn't see other fishing villages before we reached Salvador, our visit to Costa Azul had made the entire trip worthwhile.

Chapter 7

Starting Out from Mucuri

When we started our mapping job, our initial plan was to go as far south as possible in Bahia and work our way north. So far nothing about this job had worked out as we had planned. Finally, after our disastrous foray to Conde and the trip to Recife to get another truck, we were ready to try to go south again. Today our destination was Mucuri, a town near the border of Bahia and Espirito Santo. According to our map book Mucuri was a tiny little place with windswept, deserted beaches. We didn't expect to find much, but we had to start somewhere.

We were beginning to get a little experience in this travel stuff, so we weren't too intimidated by the long trip ahead of us. From Salvador to Mucuri is about 1,200 kilometers (750 miles).We planned to make the trip in two days. The idea was to drive until we got tired and then find a place to spend the night. We knew we could find a hotel or *pousada* somewhere. The map book gave descriptions of the various places in which we could find *pousada*s or hotels. (We were looking for hotels, not motels. We had been warned that in Brazil, a motel was not a reputable place to stay. The rooms in those places are usually rented by the hour, if you know what I mean.) The map book was becoming indispensable to us. Without that book we would have ended up in more pickles than we did.

This time we didn't need the map book, because we found a place right on the highway. The hotel, on the edge of a small town, was surrounded by a fortress-like wall. We checked in and went to our room to rest. Before very long our rest was interrupted by a horrible thunderstorm. I think the thunder may have been the loudest I've ever heard. Then the electricity went off. The room didn't have a patio or even a stoop, so we couldn't go outside without getting drenched or struck by lightning. All we could do was huddle in the darkness and feel sorry for ourselves. Soon, however, we heard a knock on the door. Under his dripping umbrella the desk clerk was standing in the doorway; in his hand he had a candle for us. We placed the lit candle on a saucer and were grateful for its tiny glow. The good news was that we didn't have plans that required electricity anyway. We weren't going to watch TV. The storm passed quickly and left everything feeling refreshed. Then after a little bit the electricity was restored. We went over to the restaurant and had supper.

The next day we arrived in Mucuri. The town was a major surprise. Instead of a cluster of little huts we found a thriving town with many businesses and several very nice places to stay. Mucuri was big—well beyond the specifications of our research.

The drive from Salvador had been long, but if you didn't consider the life-threatening BR 101 challenging, the trip had been easy. We drove around the town checking out things. The beaches were deserted; they looked just like the pictures in the map book. I wasn't sure why they weren't filled with people. I'm not much of a beach bum, but the ocean didn't look much different here than the ocean in Salvador did. I guess I don't know enough about beaches. We didn't see signs of fishermen either, but the town was bustling. We were especially glad to find more than one Baptist church. We checked into a nice *pousada* and made plans to drive the next day on down to the settlement of Costa Dourada. Costa Dourada is an oceanfront village right on the border between Bahia and Espirito Santo. We were determined to cover the assigned area thoroughly by starting as far south as possible.

The next morning was a dreary, rainy day, but we set out anyway. After we went a little farther south down BR 101, we turned off the highway in the direction of the ocean. The rain made the winding dirt road more difficult to travel. At least the little truck plugged doggedly along without a problem. This tough little pickup didn't cough and die. We didn't see smoke boiling from under the hood.

Mile after mile rolled away underneath us. The road had many curves and crossroads but no signs or directions. When we would encounter a fork in the road, we would pick the road that seemed the most logical to us and would keep going. We slogged through thousands of acres of eucalyptus forests that had been planted for pulp and charcoal production. We saw the loading areas in which huge piles of trimmed logs were piled as far as we could see waiting to be hauled out to paper mills or charcoal plants.

We didn't meet any cars and saw very few people. Everyone else had the good sense to stay inside. The day was gray and dreary—not a good day for a drive in the country. Only the novelty made the trip interesting, because slopping through the mud really was very miserable. The road was well-maintained, wide, and relatively free of potholes, because the lumber companies drove this way regularly.

Finally we reached our destination. The town we found at the end of that long, muddy trip was not a fishing village. In fact the place barely qualified to be a village at all. The settlement consisted of a small cluster of shuttered houses with little sign of life. As we drove down to the water's edge, we did see a couple of hardy souls out and about. The road ended on a low bluff; the ocean stretched out, violent and empty, in front of us. Down below I could see a strip of beach. I got out and quickly snapped a couple of pictures. Then we turned around and headed out. The drive had been a long one with a dismal conclusion. Unbeknownst to us, this was only the beginning. We had no idea of the things that lay in store for us.

From Mucuri we checked out some nearby towns. All of them were much too big for our research, so we moved on up the coast to the town of Alcobaça. Since we were in town during the off-season for tourists, we found a vacancy in a hotel right across the street from the ocean. Alcobaça, at least during the off-season, was our kind of place. Being in such a nice place somewhat made up for driving 100 kilometers in the rain on a dead-end road that other day.

The hotel had a second-story balcony across the front with a great view of the palms on the beach and the ocean. The next morning we had *café da manha* on the balcony while we planned our day. In the map book I found a town called Cumuruxatiba. Because the highway curved inland, this town was situated in an isolated area about 60 kilometers from the pavement. We figured scoping out Cumuruxatiba would take all day. We sincerely hoped the excursion would be more fruitful than our trip to Costa Dourada had been.

Now we were going north toward Salvador. We drove a short way up the highway and found the road to Cumuruxatiba. I use the term *road* lightly. What we found was really a twisting path full of rocks and ruts that jarred our teeth as we bounced along. I had seen such roads in the States . . . we called them *logging roads*. The only vehicles that traveled those roads were beat-up log trucks going out to get logs. This road, unlike the one to Costa Dourada, was full of holes; a better description might be *craters*. We had no idea what sort of town we would find at the end of this trek, but we kept chugging on. Once you commit yourself to a mission such as this, you can't turn back. We couldn't drive halfway and go back without knowing what we would have missed.

Covering that 60 kilometers took a long time, but a real surprise awaited us at the end of the road. This time the town wasn't a desolate community hunkering in the rain. What we found was a nice little town of about 5,000 people. It had cobblestone streets, a central plaza, and not one but two Baptist churches. We were amazed. Why and how anyone had settled in this remote town was beyond me. I figured they must have sailed in here and worked their way inland. At any rate we now knew what kind of town Cumuruxatiba was. After the arduous trip we were not eager to get back on that terrible road again.

We were cruising around and procrastinating when suddenly Van struck off across the village as though he was a man on a mission.

"Where are you going?" I asked

"Gonna get my hair cut," he replied, as he pulled up in front of the barber shop.

Hmm, I thought. *That would make the trip worthwhile.*

The barber's name was Fabio; he happened to be a Christian. While he cut Van's hair, Fabio freely conversed about his life in Cumuruxatiba. He probably never had cut a head of hair like Van's fine stuff, but he didn't comment.

While he worked, his 2-year old daughter, Jennifer, wandered in and out of the shop. He told us that living in this community was so safe, he never really worried about her. As he talked, she took a riding toy out front to where some other kids were playing. He gave her a proud, indulgent smile. When he finished lowering Van's ears, I thought, *What the heck! I'll get my hair cut, too.* That probably wasn't the wisest decision I ever made. When Fabio finished, my hair was short enough that I wouldn't have to worry about visiting a hairstylist for a long time. The trip back to Alcobaça didn't seem nearly as long as the trip out had. That is always the case. Wonder why? Next stop: Caraíva.

In this part of Brazil, BR101 runs parallel to the coast but is probably 100 kilometers inland. Roads go from the highway to the ocean. From looking at a map knowing which ones are paved and which ones are not is difficult to tell. Whenever we picked a road on the map, we never knew in real life what we would encounter. Another thing we had already discovered is that many, many little crossroads existed that were not shown on the map. Often we just followed our noses.

On the day we went to Caraíva, even the turn from the highway didn't have a sign. We just had to use the process of elimination to figure out where to turn. A young couple was waiting at a bus stop at the intersection of the road we finally picked. We asked this duo whether this road was the way to Caraíva . . . a phrase that was going to become very familiar before the end of the day. The two of them confirmed that the road indeed did go to that town. Hoping to hitch a ride they had expectant expressions as they peered into our truck. We didn't have room for them; later we would wish we *had* been able to stuff them in somewhere.

Our Portuguese still was weak, but soon we realized that we were going to have to speak to the locals. Every time we saw someone, we would stop and do our version of, "Is this the way to Caraíva?" Every time we always got the same answer: "Yes, yes. Just keep going that way." Then they would point straight ahead of us and give us a big old Brazilian smile. So we kept going that way. And going. And going.

Suddenly the road curved so sharply around the hillside that we couldn't tell where the road went. We didn't know whether the road continued or whether we had reached the edge of the world. I got out and did a little scouting. Yes, we could continue. So continue we did.

After another long 30 minutes or so we met another truck. Well, actually, the other truck was parked in the middle of a concrete crossing over a little creek. The occupants of the truck were out using their fishing poles and trying their luck. Obligingly one of the men climbed up the bank. He drove the truck off the bridge so we could cross. As we passed by, Van beeped the horn as a signal of thanks. The men stared at us. They obviously were quite surprised to see in these parts two people who clearly were foreigners.

This road seemed to go on forever. We drove another hour or two before we arrived at a group of houses. We saw a sign directing us to North Caraíva. *Hmm*, I hadn't seen that one on the map. We went that direction, since that was the closest thing all day long we had seen to a road sign. This time we didn't find a nice town at the end of the road; we didn't find a shuttered-up community either. What we found instead was a young man in a parking area with a clipboard

He told us if we wanted to cross, we could park here. We had no idea to what place we were crossing, but we weren't turning back now. We signed our names on his clipboard, paid the fee of R$10 (10 *reis*, the Brazilian unit of money), and went down to the little dock to catch our ride. Way across on the other side of the waterway all we could see were some people meandering around.

The ride turned out to be a small boat powered by a man with a pole. I was wearing a big, wide-brimmed Bahian hat. Even though I thought I was being careful, about halfway across the river my hat flew off and sailed away to land on the water behind us. The patient pole man slowly turned around. We went back to retrieve my hat.

A real town was here, although we couldn't see it from the other side. The village had been preserved to retain the character of the old days; no cars were allowed. All of the streets were sand lanes. We saw a few mule carts and lots of shops, restaurants, and *pousadas*. Besides clearly trying to attract tourists, this interesting settlement also was way bigger than "our" villages. As usual we wandered around and just looked. Van struck up a conversation with a man who was selling frozen desserts packaged in cellophane tubes. He learned that the man, João (John), was an evangelical. Van gave him a tract that he had in his pocket. They talked a few more minutes; then we moved on. Meeting João had been interesting and encouraging.

We circled around town then started back to the dock. We weren't going to be staying here. As we passed a little restaurant, we saw João talking with a friend. He was showing the tract to him, so we stopped. João had given the tract to Sidney, another Christian. In turn Sidney had shared the tract with his friend. The two Christians were excited to have the tract as a witnessing vehicle. We told them that we had a lot of tracts in our truck on the other side of the river. We would be glad to give them some. Interestingly, Sidney's job in Caraíva was to take folks in the boats back and forth across the river. He eagerly volunteered to take us back so he could get some more tracts. Once across the river we grabbed a big handful for Sidney. We gave one to the guy with the clipboard as well. The long, treacherous trip had been worthwhile. We climbed back into the truck. We drove away from North Caraíva toward the pavement—toward the tourist town of Porto Seguro.

Chapter 8

The Voyage to Maraú

When we left Caríva, we didn't go very far before we
found a paved road. On purpose we had gone into the town the
long way, because we needed know if any villages that weren't
on the map existed. We stopped in Transcoso, just south of
Porto Seguro, a popular tourist destination. Transcoso was full
of people and so were the *pousada*s. However, the owner of
one of the *pousada*s with no vacancies took us to a nearby
place that did have a room. I thought that was exceptionally
kind of her to aid the competition that way.

Transcoso is a historical vacation spot. The *pousada* we
found was tucked away just off a large park area, but the price
was very reasonable. We were able to walk to attractions such
as shops and restaurants. At the end of the street was an over-
look at the top of a flight of stairs that led to the beach far
below. The view was awesome. I could have spent several
days in Transcoso, but, unfortunately, that wasn't part of our
job.

As we traveled north from Porto Seguro, we were pleased
to see lots of Baptist churches. Baptist work in this area meant
that the people living here would have an opportunity to hear
the gospel. Finding churches made our work here simple. We
covered a lot of ground quickly. Besides finding lots of
churches, we discovered that the terrain here was different,
too. The road didn't follow the coast with wide beaches
stretching out to the ocean on one side as we had seen in many
parts of Bahia north of Salvador. In many places here the highway was on a bluff way above the ocean from where we could

see a tiny strip of beach that was inaccessible by road. Often we drove long distances without seeing any towns. Then when we found towns, they were big ones.

We passed through Ilheus going toward Itacaré, where we planned to spend the night. However, Itacaré was a disappointment to us. We found the town to be big and unappealing. We drove around for a little while and looked for a place to stay, but we didn't see anything suitable. We did pick up an erstwhile, would-be guide. He saw us sitting in the truck near the dock and looking at our map. He approached us and asked us whether we needed a tour guide. Van told him *no*. The guy didn't want to take *no* for an answer, so when we drove off, he followed us on his bicycle. When Van stopped at the intersection, the guy pulled up beside us. He told us again that he was a guide; all we needed to do was follow him. Again Van told him we didn't want a guide. His words were accompanied by vigorous head-shaking. A big problem when working in another country is the language, but you can usually communicate *no*. The word may change from place to place, but the negative head shake is highly universal. We thought we had convinced the solicitor, but a couple of blocks up the street we slowed down to make a turn.

"I don't believe this," Van exclaimed. "That guy is still following us."

I looked back. Sure enough, the poor guy was panting up the hill behind us. I was floored, but I had to admire his tenacity. By now sweat was streaming down his face.

"What part of *no* doesn't he understand?" Van asked.

One more time he caught up with us. One more time, a little more emphatically, we told him we did not want a guide. This time when he drove off, Van pushed a little more firmly on the accelerator. Finally we were free of the guy. I was glad we had left him, but part of me couldn't help feeling sorry for him. He was so determined.

Having decided that we weren't going to stay in Itacaré, I turned to the map book for help. The map book listed a number of *pousada*s on the oceanfront in the area north of Itacaré. Getting to them would involve crossing the mouth of the Gongoji River on a *balsa*, but we still had plenty of time before dark. We drove around until we found the *balsa* station. The station was in a less-desirable part of town. I was saddened as I observed the people. One was a young girl who appeared to be about 14. She was hugely pregnant. I wondered what the future held for her and her child.

From a clerk at the window we bought our tickets for the *balsa* and then went back to the truck to wait. We had to wait quite a while; while we were waiting, I got a nature call that would not be ignored. Unfortunately, when I looked around, I didn't see a store or a restaurant nearby that looked as though it was one that would have a public restroom I would want to use. At last I decided to ask the agent at the *balsa* station. I hoped maybe the station had a restroom for customers, even though the place lacked a waiting room. When I asked the agent about a restroom, she hesitated slightly before she asked me to wait a minute as she disappeared down a hallway nearby. When she returned shortly, she directed me down the hallway. This part of the building wasn't part of the *balsa* station at all; it was someone's home. Whoever lived here didn't have very much, but the place was spotless. Every effort had been made to make the best of what the people had. I felt bad intruding on them. The restroom was just off the kitchen in which an old woman was working while a child played nearby. The bathroom door was just a curtain. As I left, I thanked them profusely. I went back, humbled, to the car. Seeing that home made me realize anew just how blessed I am. I have nothing to gripe about.

Meanwhile, back at the truck, Van still was waiting for the *balsa*. The time was about 4:30 in the afternoon. The sun was beginning to set. Thankfully, the temperature was going down, too. At last the *balsa*, truly a "rustic" boat, arrived. This *balsa* was just big enough to hold the four or five vehicles waiting to board. I wasn't impressed, but at least the vessel looked seaworthy. A pair of motor boats propelled the *balsa* across the water, since the boat had no power of its own. The way the boats maneuvered to move the ferry was interesting.

By the time the ferry was loaded, the sun was low in the western sky. We had a nice evening breeze. The trip across the river was pleasant and relaxing after the long, hot wait in Itacaré; I felt happy to be out of the city. I was looking forward to getting to our hotel and resting.

As we approached the opposite side of the river, we saw several Land Rovers waiting to haul eco-tourists to high-class resorts. The Land Rovers were in a small clearing that just had one hut of some sort off to the left. All we saw were these vehicles clustered at the water's edge. We didn't see any *pousadas*. We didn't see any stores or restaurants. We didn't even see any roads. That was not comforting, but we couldn't turn back now.

When we left the *balsa*, we fell in behind a taxi that had crossed the river with us. The taxi was following the last Land Rover. We hoped its driver knew where the *pousadas* were. The "road" went through deep sand. The Land Rover and the taxi went quickly. After a short time we somehow lost track of them. Occasionally we had to drive through large puddles from the recent rains. On either side dense, jungle-like growth grew right up to the road's edge. We zipped along with Van expertly managing the poor conditions. At first the earthy smell of the surrounding woods was wonderful. For a while we enjoyed the unique adventure, but the excitement went on and on. Night was approaching. What we thought was going to be a quick, interesting jaunt through the woods to an area along a beach lined with all sorts of *pousada*s and hotels turned out to be a long, slip-sliding drive that seemed to go nowhere. All signs of civilization had disappeared. We wondered when we would find the nice places to stay the guide book promised. Sometimes we would glimpse other cars off in the distance, but basically we were traveling alone. We weren't always comfortable going through some of the places we had to cross in our tough little pickup. We thought about the taxi again. We wondered how that little car managed to go through those places. We hadn't seen that taxi in a long time. Maybe the car hadn't made all those crossings.

When we at last encountered a real gravel road, we saw a man from a big truck removing a tow rope from the front bumper of the taxi. *Where was that taxi going? How much would that fare be?* I, personally, had begun to wonder whether any of us was going anywhere! At least we were on a better road with some traffic now. We fell in behind a big dump truck. We decided the truck had to be going to a town, so we followed. We never saw the taxi or the Land Rovers again. We must have missed a turn somewhere, but I surely hadn't seen the road.

After an hour or so we entered a town of sorts. We stopped to get fuel and asked the attendant about *pousada*s. He told us about an inn right along the main road ahead of us. We were so relieved to have that treacherous trip behind us. We were eager to find a nice place for the night. The spirit of adventure had evaporated long ago.

Unfortunately, our relief was premature. We drove into "town" to find narrow streets crowded with people going up and down. We saw shabby bars and rundown restaurants, but we didn't see a *pousada* of any type—good or bad.

We drove on and followed what appeared to be the main drag. The street went up a steep hill and then curved past a huge Catholic church. This obviously was the better part of town. The street here was lined with respectable-looking houses; still we saw no hotels or inns. After making a big loop without seeing anything that remotely resembled a place to stay, we ended up back where we had started. In a situation such as this, you can do nothing but ask again. Again we were told that a *pousada* was behind a restaurant just up the street from where we were. By now we were very tired, irritated, and frustrated. Neither of us was saying much. The few signs we saw were difficult to read in the dim light. When we pulled into the restaurant we had been told about, we still had doubts. We had passed this restaurant at least three times already. Wearily we approached the server and asked whether he had a *pousada*. To our amazement he assured us that he indeed did have rooms to rent. He called his mother, an unhappy-looking, shriveled up old woman. She led us out the back of the restaurant, around the end the building, along its back side, up a narrow flight of stairs with walls on either side, and down a balcony lined with closed doors to the room at the very end. She wrestled with the key and finally opened the door. *Ta-dah!* In front of us was a cramped little room with a tiny bathroom off in the right-hand corner. A little table held a tiny, ancient TV topped with a rabbit-ear antenna. A decrepit bed occupied the center of the room. *Lovely. Charming. Much better than sleeping in the truck.* We told her we would stay.

As soon as the door closed behind her, Van ripped the covers back on the bed and inspected the sheets for foreign material. He was convinced the sheets were clean. Then we trekked back to the truck to get our stuff. We always were well-prepared, so we had lots of baggage. Besides a suitcase each for our clothes, we had the computer, another suitcase with miscellaneous paraphernalia, and "the black bag" holding maps and books. We were dreading dragging all of that through the restaurant and over the obstacle course to our room. We were blessed to learn we could drive around and park closer, but we still had to traverse the long stairs and hike to the distant room. That was quite a chore. When we got everything inside, we piled the stuff in the small spaces between the bed and the wall. Then we collapsed on the bed. Our adventure had turned into a stressful endurance challenge.

Now that we had a place to sleep, we began to think about eating. We hadn't eaten in a long time. We reversed our steps to find the restaurant again. Like thousands of other restaurants in Brazil this restaurant was a big, open space. Twenty or thirty little plastic tables covered with plastic tablecloths accompanied with plastic chairs were arranged throughout. A television at one end was tuned into the current *novella*, the Brazilian version of a soap opera. A man drinking beer was sitting at one table along the wall. We chose a table near him. Soon the proprietor approached us. Since the restaurant didn't have a menu, he described the two or three options of food available for the evening's dining pleasure. We weren't completely sure what the options were, but we decided on the *moqueca*, a type of fish soup. After the way the day had gone so far, we weren't expecting much. However, since we were not far from the ocean, we thought maybe the *moqueca* would be good. Supper turned out to be delicious and plentiful. We went back to the room well-fed and very tired.

The room had a big window that opened to the end of the building. We had been assured that mosquitoes wouldn't be a problem (yeah, right), so we swung the wooden shutters open and looked out at the street. We could see the roofs of the nearby houses and not much else. We had no idea where we really were, but at that point we really didn't much care. We certainly weren't going anywhere else that night. We were thankful to have a place to stay.

We showered and went straight to bed and straight to sleep. We slept the sleep of the just and then awoke to bright sunshine streaming in the window. Surprisingly, we had no mosquito bites.

The town that the night before we thought might be the gates of hell looked a lot different in the morning light. In the light things usually do look amazingly better. What we saw in the morning sun seemed to be a quaint little fishing town on some sort of inlet. Birds were singing. Dogs were wandering along the now-deserted street. We loaded our suitcases and then went to eat breakfast before we checked out.

Café da manha was another pleasant surprise. This breakfast was one of the best we had had in our travels. We even had fried eggs; the coffee was great.

Van went to settle our account. The room had cost a whopping R$40 (about $20). Supper had cost more than the room. The final bill was about $50. That's not bad for a room and two good meals.

We still were curious about those promised *pousada*s, so we decided to try to find them in the daylight just to see if they existed. We made the loop around by the Catholic church again and drove through the residential area. We never did find the *pousada*s, but we did find something else that put a big smile on our faces: a Baptist church.

We spent the morning driving to the nearby towns. All of them were bigger than the type for which we were looking, so we were ready to leave this fine metropolis. We were dreading the hazardous trip back. We weren't even sure we could go back. I consulted the map—yes, I still had faith in that thing. Happily, after this foray into Maraú, we didn't have to backtrack to the *balsa*. I found another route out. A road on this side of the river went back to the main highway. The map was wrong in one aspect—on the map the road was dirt, but in reality the road was paved. *Yes!*

We had been so glad to find Baptist work all along the coast south of Salvador. Because of that we had covered the area much faster than we had expected. Once we got back to BR 101, we found the highway lined with long stretches of condos, gated communities, and resorts. These places weren't home to people eking out a living fishing. When we got to Valencia, a town across the bay from Salvador, we decided to take a day off. We chose the beach town of Guaibim to kick back for a little while. Guaibim was more inviting than Maraú was. The area is a popular vacation destination for Salvadorans After our mini-vacation we caught the ferry across the Bahia dos Todos os Santos (All Saint's Bay). This ferry crossing was just a little different from the last one we had made. In the first place this boat actually was called a *ferry boat*. (In Portuguese that would be pronounced *fehr-hee bo-chee*.) I don't know what criteria are used to distinguish a ferry boat from a *balsa*, but this boat was a huge vessel that had two levels. On the top level was a large passenger lounge complete with a couple of TV's. We had a nice, relaxing voyage that ended in the mad-house of downtown Salvador traffic. Even though the traffic, as usual, was crazy, we were glad to be back for a while. Traveling was interesting and fun, but I'd learned one thing for sure: No matter how temporary, there's no place like home!

Chapter 9

Moving to Fortaleza

In less time than we had expected, we had covered the coast from Recife to the border of Espirto Santo. Now we were faced with the task of relocating to continue our work on the northern coast. We looked at the map. After we talked with our supervisors, we decided to move to Fortaleza. That would be about halfway between Recife and the western border of Maranhão.

The next job actually was to get to Fortaleza. Talking about doing this is much easier than acting. We had a couple of options for moving: (1) We could pack and ship all of our stuff as we had when we moved from Campinas, or, (2) We could pack all our things into our own truck and take them with us. To ship things would take several days to arrange. After we got everything packed and before we could leave, we would have to wait until the stuff was picked up. If we hauled our stuff ourselves, we would have to figure out how to get everything into our little truck, but we could leave sooner. Getting everything in our truck would be a trick in itself, but we really were eager to leave, so we decided to move ourselves.

First we packed all of our stuff as compactly as possible. Since a lot of our stuff had not been unpacked since we left Campinas and still was in foot lockers, getting organized didn't take long. Then we had to figure out a way to haul everything in a weather-resistant manner. We bought a sheet of black plastic that was more than six-yards long and six-yards wide. Over the truck we draped the plastic as though it was a giant shroud and began loading. Putting the baggage on the truck was like working a puzzle. We knew we could get everything in, but the stuff would fit only in a certain manner. We juggled things around until we got that accomplished. Then we folded the "flaps" up around the big pile of stuff in the back of the pickup. The result looked as though it was a huge, black Christmas present; all our package needed was a bow. At that point we were happy to have a pickup, because everything would not have fit into the SUV. After we completed the wrapping, Van began to tie things up. He was determined that the plastic be secure; he made sure nothing was going to fall out. I didn't see how anything could escape, even if it had not been tied. When he finished, ropes were lashed across the top from every direction. That sucker wasn't going anywhere unless the whole truck went. At last we were ready to go. Inside the truck we each had only a little cockpit-like area in which to sit, but everything was on board. With a last backward glance at Salvador we headed resolutely north on the now-familiar roads.

That first day we drove as far as Praia do Francês. Once before we had enjoyed staying at a place here, so we spent the night at the same hotel. Being acquainted with the owner seemed strange, because we rarely stayed in the same place twice. We weren't accustomed to knowing people when we traveled. After breakfast the next day we continued our trip.

Our friends, Rick and Jill, had moved to Campina Grande. Happily, Campina Grande was conveniently on the way. Our next stop would be at their house, at which we would stay for couple of days. For several hours we plugged away without incident and chopped off the miles bit by bit. Then that changed.

Brazil has occasional checkpoints set up by various types of government agencies. The most common agency is the

Policia Militar (Military Police). Once in a while at these checkpoints an official-looking guy in army fatigues, black combat boots, and a beret will step out, stop you, and ask for your documents. That didn't alarm us, because our documents were in order. What bothered us was that once they stopped you, they also could check anything in your vehicle. If they found a problem of any sort, they could detain you or impound your car. A Brazilian friend had warned us that the person who stopped you might invent a problem. He might say, for example, that your fire extinguisher, required in all vehicles in Brazil, was out of date. Then the man would imply that this deficiency could be overlooked for a small fee. You were more or less at their mercy. The last thing we wanted was to end up in a situation like that. We always prayed fervently that they wouldn't stop us; most of the time we just slowed to 40 kilometers per hour and eased past. Smiling didn't hurt things, but we usually did our best to avoid eye-contact. Fortunately we never had a problem at a checkpoint.

On this day we cruised merrily past a weigh station. No one stepped out to flag us down; we breathed a big sigh of relief. However, about 30 minutes later a van rapidly approached us from behind. He passed just on the crest of a hill and swooped around in front of us. He narrowly avoided our front left fender and an oncoming car. Then, not 20 feet ahead, he swerved to the right and screeched to a halt on the shoulder. I shook my fists at the driver. As we passed, I mouthed words that expressed what an idiot I thought he was. He gestured back. Then, to our horror, Van realized the van was the police! Surely we were in deep trouble now. As soon as he could safely pull over, Van stopped the truck. The police officer then drove up and stopped in front of us. He was ready to block the escape of desperate fugitives. I already had our documents in my hand. Prayers were going up.

The police officer hopped out of the van; he was followed closely by a man dressed in civilian clothes. The officer swaggered toward our truck, but the civilian-looking guy suddenly jumped back into the van as though the van had sucked him back in. My heart was thumping. I tried to remember just what I had said to this nice gentleman as we went past him. With a smile he asked for our documents. I wondered why he was so pleased. That big smile did nothing to ease my fears. Van was silent. I passed the documents and our license over to Van; he passed them on to the police officer. The officer studied them for a long time. We had been told that every state in Brazil had its own documentation, so many of the officials would have no clue about what they were seeing when we gave them our papers. That was especially true when they saw our Arkansas driver's license. Apparently, this guy was one of those clueless officials. After he looked at the papers a long time he pointed to the back of the truck.

"Your truck is loaded with lots of stuff," he smiled. "Can we take a look?"

I groaned inwardly as I thought about the yards of plastic tightly laced with more yards of clothesline.

"Opening the bindings would be difficult," Van replied. "We're Americans. We're moving from Salvador to Fortaleza."

The smile broadened into a big grin.

Now we're really in for it, I thought.

"Ah! *Americanos, neh?*" he said. He nodded his head in a knowing way as if to say *Whoopee! We're gonna get rich now!*

What he actually said was, "Well, you passed through the checkpoint a few kilometers back without stopping. When you are heavily loaded, you must stop. You might be hauling contraband or drugs." He peered into the back seat and saw the pile of suitcases.

"We're Baptist missionaries," Van stated as he tried a smile of his own. "We've been working along the coast near Salvador. Now we are moving to a new area." Smile. Smile.

Mr. Officer looked back at the documents in his hand. Then he strolled toward the back of the truck. He tugged on one of the ropes and saw how the plastic was wrapped around and around. Meanwhile, in the cab of the truck the tension was palpable. Neither of us said anything, but I thought I could detect the thumping sound of my heart! Then the police officer was back at the window; he was still smiling. I took that as a positive sign, but I wasn't sure whether the sign was positive for him or for us. Then he handed the documents back to Van.

"Between here and Fortaleza you will probably pass more checkpoints. Be sure to stop and show your documents, so they won't have to chase you down again. I don't know how many you'll pass. *Bom dia!* (Good day)."

With that he turned and sauntered back to his van, climbed in, and slammed the door. He made a u-turn and drove out of our lives with a little wave of his hand.

We just sat without moving and were hardly able to breathe. Finally, with a big sigh, Van handed me the documents. Another few shaky minutes passed before he started the engine. Once again we were under way.

"Do you realize he almost caused a head-on collision trying to stop us?" Van asked. "I saw him flying up behind us with his lights flashing, but you know how the cops are here. They always drive with their lights flashing. I didn't think it meant anything."

"I shook my fists and made faces at him when he pulled off the road!"

"How were we supposed to know that loaded vehicles were supposed to stop?"

"Did you see that other guy—the civilian-looking one? Maybe they were looking for someone in particular."

"Maybe they were looking for a truck like ours that had been stolen," Van sighed again. "Stop at every police check from here to Fortaleza. Yeah, right! Turn myself in? I don't think so."

"When he learned we were Americans, I thought we were in for it!"

"No, I think when he learned we were Americans, he knew we weren't who he was hunting. I think that's why that other guy got back in the van so fast."

"Maybe, but, whatever, I praise God that he didn't arrest us and drag us off to jail."

"Yeah, probably wouldn't have looked good for two missionaries to get hauled in for transporting 'contraband or drugs.' God was with us. Thank you, Lord!"

We drove for many kilometers before our heart rates settled back to normal. After we finally calmed down, the rest of our trip to Campina Grande was without incident. I guess that "incident" was enough for one day.

We had a great visit with Rick and Jill. We learned more about their ministry in the northeastern part of Brazil. Resting and relaxing with friends for a couple of days was nice, but soon we had to be on the road again. Rick had mapped out a route for us and assured us that his Brazilian friend had said this was the best way to go. (Yes, this is the same Rick who was our navigator in Recife.) He did warn us that the road would have some rough spots along the way. That was a good thing. We wouldn't know what to do without rough spots.

From Campina Grande we traveled several hours before we turned north on the highway that cut toward the coast. That is where we encountered said "rough spots." *Rough spots* was a huge euphemism for what we found. The road was just a series of potholes held together with patches of asphalt. Driving on this road was sort of like driving on a gigantic version of one of those plastic ring thingies that holds six packs together. We had been on primitive roads in southern Bahia, but those were way off the main drag. This was different. This was the main drag. We jolted along and at a snail's pace crept through the huge craters. At least I was able to get a good look at the surrounding area—not that I had much to see. We were passing through an area called the Agreste. The Agreste is an area between the coastal plain and the dry, rugged, desert area called the Sertão. When I looked out the window, all I could see was scrub plants, cactus, and rocks. I was hoping that, since we were away from the coast and the city, we would see some wildlife. The only wildlife we saw was an occasional lizard; even the birds seemed to be hiding out. Crossing this short section of countryside took several hours, so we arrived at Mossoró, our destination for the day, later than we had anticipated. Mossoró is a fairly large town about 30 miles from the coast. We thought finding a hotel or *pousada* for the night in such a big city would be easy, but we didn't see any. We were happy, however, to see a couple of Baptist churches. In our trusty old map book I saw a village named Tibaú situated right on the coast just a short distance away. I don't know why I still had so much faith in that book after our dreadful experience to Maraú, but I did. The book may have been misleading sometimes, but without the map book we wouldn't have any idea where to go.

We drove on to Tibaú. Saying that Tibaú is not a tourist destination is sufficient. We went up one street and down another. Finally we saw a sign for a *pousada*. This *pousada* didn't really look as though it was a place we wanted to stay, but we couldn't be too choosey. The not-too-friendly clerk led us up the stairs and down the hall to a little nook of a room tucked away in the corner of the building. The room wasn't good, but we had stayed in worse—in Maraú, for example. We took the room and settled in.

The first things we wanted were good, hot showers. We were out of luck in that department, but even the cold showers felt good. However, water from the shower ran out into the rest of the room. Anything sitting on the floor got soaked. That explained the big squeegee they had left in the bathroom. I hustled around trying to corral the water and to keep our stuff dry.

During the night we had a terrible thunderstorm. That is how we discovered that the room itself wasn't waterproof either. We slept right through the storm, but when we woke up the next morning, the floor was flooded with water from the storm. My purse and my book had gotten soaked. I was more than a little ready to get out of that place.

When we went downstairs for breakfast, we were not happy campers. We expected the same cheery welcome we had received the night before. However, this morning the clerk seemed to be a different person. Maybe a good night's rest had restored his good nature. Maybe he was a vampire. At any rate, breakfast was good, our host was affable, and soon we were seeing Tibaú in our rearview mirror. Next stop: Fortaleza.

Fortaleza was a whole new experience. Situated on the north coast of Brazil, Fortaleza is an area of beautiful beaches and lots of sunshine. Missionary colleagues Rob and Phyllis had made reservations for us at Hotel Beira Mar (Sea Side Hotel). Our only responsibility was to find the place. Again I have to admire Van's driving skill as he navigated the unfamiliar streets.

True to its name, Hotel Beira Mar is right on the beach. The hotel is a big, modern establishment with all the comforts we had been missing—Internet, TV, and phone access to the

States. God bless Rob and Phyllis. Settling in to the seventh-floor room with an ocean view overlooking a popular tourist area was pure bliss.

Our first order of business—actually, our only order of business for the time being—was to find an apartment to rent. The plan was for us to locate two or three suitable apartments to show Ed. (You remember Ed, don't you?) Then he would fly to Forteleza to approve them and finalize the paperwork.

On our first full day in Fortaleza we hired a taxi for the day to take us to the real-estate offices we had been checking out online. At the real-estate office we told the people the numbers of the properties we had liked. After taking a deposit from us they gave us the keys to five apartments. We just sat back and let Gilson, the *taxista* (taxi driver), do the driving. We enjoyed looking at the sights, but we weren't very excited about the apartments we saw. We managed to pick out three to show Ed. For lunch Gilson recommended a restaurant that served typical Northeastern food; the meal was delicious.

Back at the hotel we were thrilled to be able to use our international phone service to call home and talk to our daughters, Nancy and Marci. After all this time talking to them was such a blessing.

After we made our phone calls, we went exploring. Across the street from the hotel are lots of restaurants. A *feira* (street market) sets up every night. The boardwalk area backs up to the Atlantic Ocean. Fortaleza truly is an oceanside paradise.

We spent our days at Beira Mar looking for apartments. Gilson became our regular driver and our friend. We were amused that he took the responsibility on himself to take care of us. For example, when we went looking for used furniture, he talked to the shop owners and told them what we wanted. He would listen to the prices they quoted us. Once we were back in his taxi, he would tell us whether he thought the prices were fair or not. On more than one occasion he went with us into the apartment to take a look for himself. Having Gilson's help was nice. The way he cared for us made me think of the way Sandro had taken charge when we broke down in Conde.

At night, more often than not, we would stroll down to the *feira* and browse around. Occasionally we would buy something. We became rather addicted to the cashews that were so plentiful and cheap at the market. Mostly we just watched the people and took in the sights. We tried out various restaurants and found some really good ones. We especially enjoyed the seafood. Eating at various American fast-food chains was nice for a change, too, although we didn't do that very much.

One night on the "strip" we met a guy who spoke English We got to know Pedro because he heard us speaking English and struck up a conversation. After that first encounter we would run into him occasionally. We told him we were missionaries. One night we gave him a tract. That particular night he was going to a gigantic concert being held just down the street. One of the most popular Brazilian singers was going to be performing; thousands of people were expected to attend. When we gave him the tract, he glanced over the leaflet and stuck the paper in his pocket. The next time we saw him, he asked us for another tract. When he had gone to the concert that night, someone had picked his pocket. The thief took the tract we had given him. I guess whoever got the tract got an extra blessing. I wonder what kind of seed was planted.

Meanwhile, our apartment search continued. We would find a nice apartment that was in a yucky location or a yucky apartment that was in a great location. At least we had a few for Ed to see. We had our choices narrowed down and ready when he arrived to finalize things for us. All of us, plus Gilson, went back to the real-estate office we had visited. We got the keys; Gilson took us around to the various apartments.

By the time we got back to the office, we had pretty much decided on one. When we sat down with the real-estate agent, Ed explained that our mission was headquartered in Brasilia. He said he would be signing all the necessary papers and making arrangements for payment. That was when the agent decided to break the news to us that since we were a not-for-profit organization, he could not rent to us. Suddenly after days of apartment-hunting we were back at ground zero. We were all shocked.

As soon as we left the office, we began to discuss an alternative plan of action. Van said he had seen a "for rent" sign on a post down the street, so we went to check that out. We got a phone number. Then we drove around looking for similar signs.

Gilson said he knew of a place that had temporary rentals. He suggested we go to that place. Fortaleza has many tourists, so many apartments for short-term rental are available, too. At the first place the agent didn't have anything. I saw another rental agency across the way, so we went to that store. This agency had an apartment furnished with everything except a washer. We hurried over to take a look. After we saw the apartment, we knew the place was just what we needed. Ed and Gilson thought we could get a washer thrown into the deal, too. Ed had to leave the next day, but he was able to get the ball rolling first. He could manage the details from Brasilia; besides, we had Gilson.

Before we moved in, the agent needed to go with us to assess the condition of the apartment. She had a list of all the apartment's contents. As we walked through the place, we noted everything on the list and removed a few objects. Gilson stayed nearby the whole time to make sure the agent treated us right. God truly does work in mysterious ways. Just when we needed help, He provided this great guy for us.

After two weeks at Beira Mar, we said goodbye to our friends at the hotel and checked out. Even though we had been busy, staying in the hotel had been a wonderful departure from our constant travel. Our truck, still loaded, was waiting in the garage. The truck hadn't been moved since the night we arrived.

Our new home was on the 14th floor of a highrise apartment building. I never would have imagined I would ever live in such a place, let alone like the place. The day really did seem sort of like Christmas when we unwrapped our big present. Seeing our stuff again after all this time lifted our spirits. The apartment was tiny, but, once we were unpacked, our place seemed as though we were returning home for the first time since we had left Campinas and language school.

Chapter 10

Working from Fortaleza

Once we were established in Fortaleza, we were eager to get back to work. The SUV still was in Brasilia, but we were supposed to get the truck back just any old time. The head gasket was being replaced. We were expecting the SUV to be like new when the truck finally got to Fortaleza. Meanwhile, we had the little pickup we had gotten in Recife. We were quite happy with that one.

We had completed the stretch of coastline from Espirto Santo to Recife. Now we would begin working from Recife to the western border of Maranhão. We had to plan a strategy of how to accomplish that. We decided to begin by working east toward Recife. From Fortaleza to Recife is a distance of about 1,000 kilometers, but you start the longest journey with the first step.

At first we planned to drive right along the coast as we had done in Bahia, Seregipe, and Alagoas, but soon we discovered that wasn't going to be possible. The roads along the coast out of Fortaleza deadended at different bodies of water. We would take off down one and hope to find a bridge or a *balsa*, but we then we would have to backtrack. Finally we found a route heading east through the towns of Aquiraz, Pindoretama, and Cascavel. We immediately realized that this part of the country had much less Baptist work. We didn't see any Baptist churches. In fact, we didn't see many churches of any sort. We soon found two small fishing villages that had no evangelical work.

Along the way we took advantage of the opportunity to see some of the popular attractions in the area. Of course the main attraction was the ocean and its surrounding dunes. Much of the northern coast is covered with sand dunes. Once, when we were exploring an area off the main road toward the coast, we found ourselves at the end of a road surrounded by some huge dunes. We saw a trail going up the side of one of them, so we decided to climb that one. For miles around we seemed to be completely alone without anyone else. We started climbing and hadn't gone far when we realized we were being followed. Apparently the young man behind us had just materialized from thin air. Although we were a little uncomfortable and suspicious with his being behind us, we continued climbing but stayed alert to what he was doing. When we reached the top, we had a beautiful view of lagoons and sand dunes. The climb was worthwhile.

As soon as we stopped, the young man approached us. We eyed him warily, but he turned out to be a sort of self-appointed tour guide. He told us all about the things we were seeing. Then he offered to take a picture of us together. After he clicked a few frames, he started walking in the opposite direction with my camera in his hand.

Uh-oh, I thought. *Giving him my camera wasn't a good idea.*

I was sure that my camera and the photos on it were gone for good, but after just a few strides he turned and gave the camera back to me. *What a relief.* I had learned a lesson.

He continued to show us around. I was surprised when he led us up a really steep dune. He was asking a lot of this old woman. I was hoping I could make the climb without sliding back down. At the time I didn't know that the sliding was on the other side. After we reached the crest, we just sort of slid down on our backsides. Going down was a lot more fun than going up—sort of like sledding minus the snow and the sled. We ended up right at the truck.

That night we stayed in a rustic *pousada* right on the beach. The *pousada* was owned by a French man named Bruce. Bruce was a wind-tossed, sunbleached, beach bum of a man in his 30s who taught kite-surfing lessons. Kite-surfing is immensely popular in this part of the country. We had seen lots of people sailing out across the water. Kite-surfing appears to be a really strenuous sport that requires a lot of upper body strength. I liked watching people kite-surf. When Bruce told us that he had a student who was 74-years old, I was tempted to try the sport.

As often was the case because of the time of the year, we were the only guests he had that evening. Because of that we were able to spend time visiting with him. He told us we were the first Americans he had ever had stay in his *pousada*. As we talked, he told us about how he had ended up in Brazil. He said he never would go back to France. I wondered whether one day I might possibly have the same sentiments about the United States.

That night we slept with the windows open. Not far away we could hear the surf crashing. Even though I'm definitely not a beach bum, I could understand the lure of this kind of life.

The next day we stopped in another small town to inquire about churches. We immediately attracted a crowd. In these parts strangers were rare. Within a minute the one man at our truck window had mushroomed into at least a dozen interested bystanders. When they found out our mission, they were more than eager to share with us. They insisted that we go into their fish-processing plant for a tour. The processing plant had just been finished; everything was new and sparkling. After we toured the plant, the people had to show us the restaurant/bar.

One man, straight from the sea, had an eel in his fishing bucket. He proudly held the fish up for a photo op. Obviously, they were fishermen, but the big town didn't have a Baptist church.

From that town we went on to the tourist town of Canoa Quebrada (Broken Canoe) to spend the night. Several decades ago this town was invaded by hippies; they have remained. We found many interesting things in Canoa Quebrada. The main street, Broadway, goes from the inland street to the ocean. Restaurants and shops of all kinds line the street; the street has been converted into a pedestrian mall. At the end of the street is a long flight of stairs leading down to the beach. We stood at the head of the stairs and looked out over the panoramic view of the ocean and the people on the beach. When we turned to leave, we were surprised to see, right in the middle of all that tourist stuff—right where we least expected to see one—the First Baptist Church of Canoa Quebrada! What a blessing. Canoa Quebrada was to become one of our favorite stopover points as we worked in the area east of Fortaleza.

Although we loved going to the town, getting to Canoa Quebrada was a big problem. This time the problem wasn't miles of muddy roads with huge rocks; the problem was about 10 miles of formerly asphalted highway full—I mean chock full—of potholes big enough to hide an 18-wheeler. In one community through which we had to pass, the road was so bad that everyone just drove on the shoulder because the shoulder was so much smoother. We marveled at how the Brazilian government could let the road to such a popular place be so neglected.

In this part of Brazil, BR 304 is the main highway; this highway is as scary as is its southern cousin, BR 101. The potholes in this road are numerous; the road is a regular obstacle course. Dodging the trucks that were dodging the potholes added a level of difficulty to driving. At night you could see the oncoming headlights bobbing back and forth. The lights served as a warning for bad roads ahead like a mobile light-house. Too bad Van wasn't getting points for his driving skill. Thankfully after 100 kilometers or so the road did get better.

We crossed into the state of Rio Grande do Norte and finished up the day ducking in and out of all the small villages along the coast. Then we headed to the larger town of Grossos in search of a place to spend the night. Grossos is not like Canoa Quebrada. After a long search we found a place with vacancies, but the hotel was right across the street from a restaurant/bar. That concerned us, so we asked the employees whether the restaurant got loud at night. They nodded glumly. They suggested that we take the *balsa* across to Areia Branca, because we probably could find a place in that town. Oh, goody, another *balsa*. However, this seemed like a reasonable idea, so we drove on down to the dock to wait. We took advantage of the waiting time to kick back and rest a bit. I even slept a little. In these situations Van never sleeps.

After a while people began gathering for the *balsa*. Most of them were on foot or riding bicycles. Then a big pickup loaded down with fruit and building supplies pulled up and parked in front of us. When the *balsa* finally arrived, we were less than thrilled. The boat was tiny and dilapidated-looking. I contemplated the body of water we were going to cross and the boat on which we would make the crossing. What I saw made me distinctly uncomfortable. The fact that we had just heard about a ferry sinking in the Amazon didn't help matters. Oh, and have I mentioned that Van doesn't swim?

Because the boat was so small and the other truck was so big, that truck was loaded first. I guess the boatmen thought they could scrunch us in better that way. When our truck was squeezed in behind the bigger one, the *balsa* was completely full. The ramp of the *balsa* was closed snuggly against our back bumper to keep the truck from rolling off. No, I didn't feel good about this trip at all.

For safety's sake all riders have to be out of their vehicles during the *balsa*'s transit. As soon as we were out of the truck, I commanded Van to find the life jackets. We located them and settled ourselves directly underneath so that they would be handy in case we went down. The crossing was very scary; disappointment waited on the other side. Once again we didn't find rows of *pousada*s as we had expected. The scene was much like Maraú all over again except, praise God, here we saw an actual town and the roads were paved.

We took off down the main drag along the coast until we found a nice *pousada*. Much to our dismay the inn was full. That was one of the few times we encountered no vacancies. That day must have been a holiday of some sort.

Brazil has tons of holidays. Brazilians like to party; they take advantage of every opportunity to do so. After looking around a little more, we decided to enlist the help of a motorcycle taxi driver to help us find a *pousada*. A motorcycle taxi is just what the name sounds like: a man who, for a fee, takes people from point A to point B on his motorcycle. I didn't plan to ever actually ride a *moto-taxi*, but we knew one of those drivers would be familiar with all the places to stay. We asked the next one we saw whether he could help us. He led us to three *pousada*s. Two of them were full; the third one reeked of the smell of mothballs. Van absolutely cannot abide the odor of mothballs. (In Brazil, mothballs often are used as air-fresheners. They're also often found in urinals, or so I've been told.)

The *moto-taxista* was out of places. He suggested that we go on down the coast to Ponta do Mel (Honey Point). He thought that we could surely find a place to stay in Ponta do

Mel. We followed him to the turnoff, paid him, and struck out on our own again. By now night had fallen; we were still on the road. I hated being in this situation. We really tried to avoid being on the road after dark, but this wasn't the first time we had found ourselves in this position. I suspected this wouldn't be the last time.

Out first impression of Ponta do Mel was not good. We drove up and down the one or two poorly lit streets but didn't see a sign of a *pousada*, hotel, or even a room to rent. We wondered why the *moto-taxista* thought this would be a good place to look for a place to stay. We were beginning to feel a little bit desperate. A woman sat on a corner; we stopped to ask her about hotels.

"*Oh, lá embaixo!* (Oh, there. Down below.)," she said as she pointed to the unlit road leading down the hill.

We looked in the direction she indicated and were not encouraged by what we saw. Oh, well, once again we were in too far to turn back now.

"*Lá embaixo*" we found a nice *pousada*. The owners were proud of their place, too. The price was way out of our range, so we continued looking. Finally, with the moon rising over the ocean, we found a *pousada* at the end of the beach.

"Do you have a vacancy?" we asked.

The clerk smiled and nodded. Success at last.

"Can we take a look?" we asked, as if that really mattered now.

He grabbed a key. Then, of course, he proceeded to lead us up a long steep flight of stairs and down a long hall to the room at the very end. I would have been surprised if he had shown us a room that was not remotely situated. He opened the door; we took a quick peek. The room would have to be really, really bad for us to leave. Even the thought of lugging all our baggage up all those stairs didn't deter us. Happily, the room was a good one.

When we went down to get our stuff out of the truck, Van decided to turn the truck around and back up near the gate to make unloading easier. The sad thing was he didn't see the pole—the pole that he hit as he backed up. After maneuvering traffic in São Paulo, Salvador, Recife, and Fortaleza—after driving thousands of kilometers across the wilds of Brazil dodging potholes and traffic along its dangerous highways, Van was brought down by a pole! That was a fitting end to a stressful day. He got out and strolled around to the back of the truck to take a look. Then he laughed. He laughed right out loud.

After we took all of our luggage up to the room, we went in search of something to eat. We hadn't eaten since breakfast. Eating just hadn't been a priority that day. Now we were ravenous. We didn't remember seeing any restaurants, so we started out by asking the clerk at the desk. For a few minutes he pondered. Then he told us the town had a *lanchonete* (what we'd call a *hamburger joint*) just up the way a little. *Yummy.* A greasy burger was just what I had in mind.

We drove back up the beach to the first street and quickly located the place he had mentioned. Finding the *lanchonete* was easy, since the joint was the only place we saw that was open. The place served sandwiches and snacks. Right away we realized this was going to be another learning opportunity. This was not the kind of place in which we usually ate, mainly because we didn't really know how or what to order.

The diner was situated on a corner. Two sides had shutters that could be lowered when the place was closed. Two or three of the ever-present plastic table-and-chair sets were on the sidewalk. We walked up to the counter and tried to look as though we knew what we were doing. Ordering wasn't as difficult as we had thought, because the selection was small. We asked for two ham-and-cheese sandwiches and juice. While we were placing our order, we noticed that the little shop had Bible verses and religious slogans posted all around.

"Are you a Christian?" we asked the man at the counter.

"Oh, yes," he replied enthusiastically.

"Well, we're Baptist missionaries. Do you have a Baptist church in this town?"

"*Hmm.* Baptist," he considered. "No. We don't have a Baptist church here, but we have a Seventh-day Adventist church, a Presbyterian church, and a Methodist church besides the Assembly of God and the Catholic church. I'm a member of the Assembly. So are my children," he said with a broad smile as he indicated the kids gathering around us as we talked. "I'm a preacher at our church," he beamed. "So are they."

We looked at the child preachers. *What an interesting concept.*

We sat down at the table on the sidewalk; the kids hovered around us. They obviously were enchanted to have real, live Americans in their midst. The dad, who had disappeared briefly to start our sandwiches, returned.

"They sing at the church," he said, still smiling. "Would you like to hear them sing?"

We looked at each other. *Wow, live entertainment and everything.*

"Of course. We'd love to!"

They quickly found their music sheets, perched on the chairs and tables close by, and began singing. They really were quite good. When they finished the first song, we applauded heartily, so they launched into another one. From inside the *lanchonete* Dad would shout out a loud "Hallelujah!" every now and then to encourage them and to stay engaged. They were so beautiful. I ran to the truck to get the camera, because

I had to have a record of this. After I clicked off several shots, the smallest boy walked over to look at the one I had taken of him. He was enthralled and grinned up at me. He was about 2- or 3-years old. When he smiled at me, the others told us that he didn't talk. On the spot I decided that somehow one day I would get a print of that photo back to him.

The sandwiches arrived and the concert ended. As we were getting ready for bed that night, we talked about how amazing our God is. He always takes care of us. We had been in some tricky situations; He had led us through each of them. Today had been no exception.

The next morning was a bright, sunshiny day. I wanted to take a walk on the beach, so we went about half a mile looking for shells. I found several sand dollars. Finding complete sand dollars always was exciting to me. After our stroll we had to hit the road again.

According to the map the road ended just a little way on down the beach, but we went that way anyway to check out some villages we saw on the map. We were delighted to find a brand-new asphalt road running right along the oceanfront. Maybe we would be able to drive from here right on down to the next town after all. The day was gorgeous. The ocean was on one side, the sand dunes stretched out on the other, and, best of all, the road was great. After a while the road turned inland. We zipped along through empty land. We thought the new road would cut miles off our travel.

After we had gone 25 kilometers or so, we encountered a huge pile of sand right across the road. Sometimes this sort of thing is meant as a roadblock. Other times sand or other material is in the road simply because that was where the workers stopped working. This time the sand was a roadblock. We eased up to the sand to see if we could get around. That was impossible, but we could see why the road was blocked. Not

200 yards ahead the road was completely washed out. Just gone. The recent flooding had swept the road away. We again were faced with a difficult decision. Should we backtrack to Grossos and go the long way around, or did we look for a shortcut? Being the conservative, timid people we are, we opted to look for a shortcut. We turned around and took the first road off the highway. Following our noses we drove along, since at the time we didn't even have a compass, let alone a GPS. We drove and drove and drove without seeing any sign of civilization. All we saw on every side was acres of scrub brush. We didn't even see the donkeys that are so common here. Besides everything else, the truck had started making some terrible noises. The sound made us think the whole front end might fall out at any moment. That did nothing to ease our fears. At last we emerged in what appeared to be a flooded lake area. The road wound around the lake bed, so we did, too. Just as we were about to get really discouraged, we topped a hill. Way in the distance we could see a town. At least we were headed somewhere, even if we weren't sure where we would be when we got there. Seeing the town was like seeing a light at the end of a tunnel. We prayed that the light wasn't another train.

The road turned from dirt to blacktop. When a family of pigs crossed the road in front of us, we knew we had arrived. A little farther down the road we saw a sign that confirmed we had reached our objective. *Yes!* Our shortcut had taken us only a couple of hours of literally wandering in the wilderness.

Now we had to find a bridge to cross the river so we could go back to the ocean. Going back toward the ocean after working so diligently to get away from the sea seemed ironic. Fortunately going back was a lot easier than going inland had been. In just an hour or so we were back driving along the coast not far from where we had started out that morning. As soon as possible we found a place to spend the night and stopped.

We had become really concerned about the truck. This vehicle which had served us so well now was making such loud noises in the front end that people turned and stared at us as we passed. Van claimed that women would grab their children and run for home when they heard us moving down the road. We were going to have to go back to Fortaleza to get the truck fixed or risk being stranded on the road again. When on our way home we limped into the hotel in Canoa Quebrada, the lady working at the desk hurried out to meet us as we parked.

"Did you have a wreck?" she asked with concern all over her face. "I heard the horrible noise your truck was making when you turned in."

Yes, we definitely had to get *Little Champ*, as I had nick-named our trusty vehicle, to the shop.

Since the noise was in the front end, we were hoping maybe the problem was something simple such as shocks. On our way into Fortaleza we passed a mechanic's shop that looked as though it was a good, reputable place, so we stopped to get the truck checked out. Now was as good a time as any. The mechanic took a quick look and then told us we would need to bring the truck back the next day. He couldn't say for sure what the problem was, but the noise wasn't caused by the shocks.

Before we got the truck repaired, we had to get estimates to turn in to Ed. Since a shop happened to be across the street from where we lived, taking the truck to that shop to get an estimate as well as from the shop we had already visited seemed like a good idea. Besides, this shop would be real handy.

We took the pickup over early the next morning. The news

94

was not good. The mechanics told us that the entire front end had to be replaced. The estimate for the repair was enormous. The estimate from the first place, while still large, was less expensive. Van made an appointment with this shop for the following week. With the broken truck we were going to be grounded for a while. That was nothing new.

Besides running around trying to get the repairs done on the truck, we also were continuing to work on getting our visas extended. Although while we were in Salvador we had managed to get a short extension, we had to register with the federal police again when we moved to Fortaleza. Now we were trying to get an open-ended extension that would be good until we got our permanent visas. The man with the federal police in Fortaleza was more understanding than the man in Houston had been, but the task still was difficult. Thankfully, Gilson had gone with us the first time, but after that we tackled the job by ourselves.

At last we thought we had everything in order. We paid all the fees and filled out the forms for the extension. The man took the completed forms and began to read them. With baited breath we sat. He read to the very last line. Then he hit a wall. We had no business address in Fortaleza. We had to have a business address here, or he couldn't sign the papers. We tried to explain, but he just kept saying *no*. Finally we called the mission office so the mission's attorney could better explain our situation. While the man talked to the attorney, we could hear his end of the conversation; his end didn't sound good. He hung up and shook his head as he looked at the forms again. I knew that this would be our last chance. If he didn't sign the documents now, I didn't know what we could do. I was on the verge of tears. The man just kept staring at the paper and shaking his head. I just knew he wasn't going to sign them.

Even though my desperation must have shown on my face when he looked up at me, he still was full of indecision. Then all of a sudden he let out a big sigh and signed the paper in a rush! *Hallelujah!* Van was persuaded that my "poor, pitiful, woman-in-distress look" is what convinced him. I didn't care why. We had our extension!

Getting the truck repaired took a long time, because we had to get estimates. The Brazilian Labor Day holiday fell right in the middle of our pursuit of estimates, too. That didn't help matters. The good news is that we had gotten to visit with Rick and Jill when they visited a resort near Fortaleza for a vacation; now the truck was much better. Little Champ no longer was making dreadful noises. After about 10 days at home we were ready to go out again.

Chapter 11

Galinhos

After our sojourn in Fortaleza while the truck was being repaired and we were wrestling with the federal police, we went back to the place at which we had stopped in our work and prepared to continue. This time we didn't take the *balsa* to Grossos or the scenic route through the wilderness. We went directly to Macaú and began working. We eased along the coast and investigated the towns. We did not find many churches or much Baptist work.

On the second day when we started to look for a place to spend the night, we were in an area that had few towns. I looked in the trusty old map book. I saw a town, Galinhos, that appeared to be large enough to support a *pousada* or two. The write-up indicated a couple, so we headed for that place. You won't be surprised to learn that what we encountered wasn't what we expected.

To get to Galinhos you drive way out to the end of a flat peninsula. The terrain is so flat that at times the car seems to be traveling on the water. Then the road just ends in a parking lot. On one side is a big building that looks as though it is a terminal or something. When we pulled in, a young man with a clipboard emerged from the building. He asked us whether we wanted to cross. *Hmm.* As I recall, we had had a similar experience in south Bahia. We looked at each other and shrugged our shoulders. *Why not?* The guy assured us that we would find places to stay on the other side, so we lugged all our stuff down to a boat at the end of a long, wooden pier. We left the truck abandoned in the parking lot and hoped the vehicle would still be there when we returned. However, this time we weren't nearly as concerned about that as we had been in Pacatuba.

The boat was a small craft with an engine house in the middle. Traversing the waterway took almost an hour. When we pulled up to a pier on the other side, taxis were waiting. However, these were no ordinary taxis. They were carts pulled by mules. We looked around in the growing darkness. We didn't see cars anywhere, so at random we picked a cart and told the driver that we needed to find a place to stay. He nodded, picked up the reins, and made a noise that sounded like a desperate attempt to dislodge a bone from his throat. The mule recognized the sound as *"Go-o-o-o-o-o-o!"* He went.

The driver took us to the nicest place in town. We went in to take a look around. The place was very nice indeed.

"How much?" Van queried.

The clerk considered a moment; he obviously wondered how much he could get out of these "wealthy" Americans.

"R$200," he finally responded.

I turned to see what Van thought, but he was gone. He didn't even reply to the inflated price.

I met him back at the cart just as he was instructing the driver to take us to a less-expensive place. Of course, the less-expensive *pousada* was a little less posh than the first one was. Actually, the place was a lot less posh than the first one. In fact, this *pousada* was less posh than almost anywhere else we had stayed. This place consisted of a few rooms set up in someone's back yard, but we would be here only for one night. We knew we could stand one night. We were tough. The price was right.

Once we settled in, the next thing on our agenda was supper. However, when we asked about restaurants, we got a puzzled silence.

98

Hmm, the female owner of the *pousada* seemed to be thinking, *How odd that these people want food.*

Her reaction didn't make us happy. We really were hungry.

"Do you like fish?" she asked. "I can fry some fish for you."

"Yes. Fish would be good." Any port in a storm . . . .hence the reason we were at her lovely establishment.

She fried up some small fish. Then from somewhere she produced some rice and beans. We ate on her back patio. The meal was most congenial and relaxing—more like supper with a friend than dinner out. We really enjoyed chatting with her.

After we ate, we went back to our room across the sandy yard. A hammock was on the porch, so Van stretched out to rest a bit while I went to try out the shower. The bathroom had no hot water, but on the northern coast of Brazil that's not as bad you might think. I grabbed the soap and began trying to work up a lather. I rubbed and rubbed. Finally I got a little foam. When I was rinsing off, I got a taste of the water. The water was almost as salty as the ocean itself was. That explained the lack of bubbles.

The next morning I opened the shutters to see where we were. Since we had arrived after dark, we had only a vague idea of the area. Looking through the window I could see acres of sand dunes with clear pools scattered around. A broken-down fence snaked across the sand. A bony horse browsed around trying to find something to eat, but the sun was shining brightly. The day was beautiful. Since we had traveled all this way, we thought we might as well take in the sights of Galinhos.

We hired the same mule driver who had chauffeured us the night before. He showed us around town. We saw one old dune-buggy-type car and a tractor but no other motor vehicles. He told us that this small town had two Assembly of God churches but no Baptist church. Then we went down the beach to the lighthouse. No one else was about that morning: no fishermen, no swimmers, no kite-surfers. All we saw was a couple of horses and a few birds wandering around. As we went along, I noticed lots of dead fish lying on the sand. When I looked closer, I realized they were flying fish. The driver said they "flew" in during high tide and were stranded when the water receded. The beach was beautiful but desolate. The surf was crashing wildly. Dark clouds loomed on the horizon; they framed the lighthouse at the edge of the water.

After our morning outing we had to get back to work. We packed everything up and then hauled our stuff down to the dock. Thankfully Little Champ still was sitting in the parking lot just as it had been the night before.

Chapter 12

Stuck on the Beach

Rio Grande do Norte is a very beautiful part of Brazil. Its beaches are beginning to attract tourists, but right now many large stretches are undeveloped. Many of the beaches we saw were just as they had been when the first Europeans arrived four centuries ago: windswept, wild, and wonderful. On this particular day we already had visited several villages. Now our destination was Tibau do Sul, where we were planning to spend the night. The area in which we traveled, a community known as Barreta, was well settled and showed distinct signs of housing developments in the making. Looking at the map we could see an inlet or bay of some sort between us and Tibau do Sul. Unless a bridge or something we didn't know about existed, we would have to go all the way out to BR 101 to drive around. That looked like a trip of 100 to 150 kilometers. We would like to avoid that if we could.

We were just sort of cruising around looking, because sometimes we had discovered roads on the ground that weren't in our map book. We saw a sign that said *balsa*. That would work. A *balsa* would save miles. Sometimes *balsas* proved to be fun! (Really! I could think of a *couple* that had been fun.) We stopped at the crudely lettered sign, but we saw no sign of a *balsa* or even a loading ramp. All we saw were two young guys hanging out and eager to give directions.

Van lowered the window. He smiled at them.

"How do we get to the *balsa*?" he asked.

A big smile greeted Van in return. The guy pointed to a path through a small hump of sand to our left.

"Right through that gap," he said. He was still grinning like the Cheshire cat.

We looked to the place he pointed; then we looked at each other. Didn't look like any *balsa* approach we had ever seen; by now we had seen several. The hump was just high enough to obscure the ocean and beach on the other side.

"I don't think so," we said to each other without saying anything.

Van looked at the guy and shook his head.

"*Acho que não* (I don't think so)," he said to the Brazilian as he started raising the window.

"No, no! Wait!" the Brazilian said. "You really can go that way to catch a *balsa*. Once you get on the beach, you just drive down to where the *balsa* ramp is."

We looked at each other again; we still were not convinced.

"No. I don't think we'll try that," Van said. Again he began to raise the window.

"But we have pictures. Look!" the guy said. He held out a photo album that displayed a small, two-wheel drive car tooling along the beach.

We looked at the pictures. We had driven on beaches before. We knew that using them as roads was not uncommon, but that entrance looked dubious.

The Brazilian saw us flinch. *Not good*. He thrust the album closer. He said that if that little car could make the trip, surely this fine, four-wheel drive vehicle we were driving could manage. "Look how broad the beach is. You'll save many kilometers," he said as he still grinned engagingly. We hesitated. We shouldn't have, of course, but we did. He leaped into the gap and began explaining how far the drive was around by the highway. He expounded about how much time we would save if we took the *balsa*.

Finally Van cautiously said, "OK. I'll take a look."

We backed up enough to turn into the little path. Things didn't look promising, but if we didn't like what we saw, we could just turn around and go on our way, right? All we were going to do was take a little peek. We eased through the gap onto the beach and made a right-hand turn. Immediately we knew this never would work. I don't know what beach was in the pictures that guy had shown us, but this scrawny strip of sand we now viewed was nothing like the pictures.

Van pushed the gear shift into reverse to leave. His eyes widened. When he revved the motor, he didn't have to say anything. We were stuck! In the blink of an eye we had gotten stuck! Before we could say, "Let's get out of here", we had gotten stuck! He put the truck into four-wheel drive, but that succeeded only in digging us in a little deeper. My mouth suddenly went dry. I looked past him to the wide Atlantic Ocean just the other side of his window. The pictures had shown a wide expanse of beach, but right here, right now, maybe 30 feet of sand was between us and the deep blue sea. Although that sea was making its daily trip inland, we weren't going anywhere. Van tried the things guys know to do to get a truck unstuck: rocking back and forth from first to reverse to begin, then getting out and rocking side to side to try to get some footing. His efforts were useless. In fewer than 60 seconds I went from skeptical to frantic—plus I was mad! Those guys had just tricked us into this to make a little money. Here we were going to make IMB history by taking a road trip across the Atlantic. As if on cue our Brazilian friends appeared over the horizon.

"Oh, my goodness," their expressions seemed to say, "Do we have a little problem? Well, we know just the guys to help you out. You're in luck."

Van was stoic about the situation. His attitude was that we

were here, so now we had to figure out how to get out of here. My attitude was a little different. I was pacing up and down and running my hands through my hair while I stared as the ocean inched its way towards the driver's door.

In a situation such as this, women usually are ignored as having nothing useful to contribute and not much muscle. That was perfectly fine with me, but I couldn't just stand by and watch. I decided to leave the problem to the guys. I grabbed the camera and snapped a quick shot before I struck off to do some serious prayerwalking. I took one backward glance as I left. The waves were crashing just seaward of the driver's side and then rolling jauntily under the truck as they tried to suck the thing back into the ocean with them. The sand was getting that soggy look. The men were doing their best to dislodge the truck. I was doing my thing by "getting out of Dodge", as the saying goes.

Filled with emotion I stalked off down the beach. Part of me was angry at the Brazilians for luring us into this trap. Part of me was angry at us for falling for their ploy against our better judgement. A third part of me was horrified at the thought of the truck drifting off to Africa on a mission trip of its own. What worried me most was not losing the stuff we had in the truck. That was not worth much anyway. My big worry wasn't losing the truck. A nine-year-old pickup couldn't be worth much either. What haunted my thoughts and prayers was how on earth we were going to explain how our truck ended up in the ocean. *What were we going to say to Ed?* Even the thought of that filled me with humiliation. I walked rapidly away from the truck in the direction we were supposed to have been able to drive. A couple of hundred feet down the beach the ocean dug sharply into the sand and effectively cut the beach in two. Right, we could drive down the beach! I was praying earnestly that God would salvage the situation, but at the same time I had to fight my resentment about being in this position in the first place.

For several long minutes I was afraid even to look back for fear of what I might see. I just hoped Van would have the foresight to grab a few things out of the truck before he waved goodbye. Then I plucked up my courage and started walking back. One of the Brazilians had run off somewhere and found a long, thick board that he had managed to push under a wheel. Just as I got close, the pickup lurched forward amid a flurry of sand and dashed past me down the short stretch of beach. My heart lurched, too. "Thank you, Lord. Thank you, Lord," I kept repeating over and over. I have not experienced many times in my life in which I have been more flooded with relief than at that moment. The guy driving the truck made a big, flourishing loop and returned for us. I got in the back seat. Everything was covered with sand. As we flew off down the beach, more sand flew in the open front window. I have to admit I didn't much care. The truck was moving again but not out to sea. The Brazilian seemed to be having a great time. He was grinning from ear to ear. I think he had had some anxious moments, too.

"The four-wheel drive isn't working well," he kept saying. *Well, duh!* I thought.

We managed to edge past the point of my desperate prayer with the left wheels flirting with the waves. Then we swung inland to a ramp-like entrance to the beach. I realized that if we had entered here, we would have had a plain view of the beach. We never would have left the road. *Oh, well, nothing to do about that now.* We went back to the place at which we first had encountered the scammers (as I had taken to thinking of these Brazilians). I spent my time brushing sand out of my flip-flops, off my legs, and out of the truck while Van paid the men 50 *reais* for their help.

"Help," I snorted to myself. My attitude definitely needed an adjustment, but I did my best to keep my mouth shut. Anyway, now that our daily adventure was over, we set out for Tibau do Sul again. This time we went the long way around. For a while we drove in silence. We both were lost in our own thoughts. Then we began to rehash every detail of the episode the way you do after something like that happens. *What if we had . . .? Why did we . . .? Those guys were . . .! How could we have been so gullible?* Of course all that introspection didn't change a thing. We had a long way to go. Now we were very tired physically besides being mentally washed out. At around six in the evening we arrived at Tibau do Sul. As usual we headed toward the beach to look for a place to stay. As we went along, I saw a sign that read *balsa*. I had to know.

"Stop, Van. Pull over right here. I'm going to see where that *balsa* goes." He looked at me like I had two heads. He had had all he wanted of *balsas* for the day, but he obligingly pulled over. I hopped out and ran into the little station.

"Where does this *balsa* go?" I fairly well demanded of the clerk.

"Why, it goes to Barreta," he replied. I stared at him with my mouth open.

Well, I'll just be, I thought. *They were telling the truth after all. Lord, forgive me.*

Chapter 13

The Road through the Woods

When we hit the road this time out, we would be making our first venture into the state of Paraiba. Despite our recent ordeal on the beach we fearlessly turned off the highway and headed toward the coast. Once we left the highway, where we were driving could not really be considered a road. We used the four-wheel drive all the time, even though after our adventure on the beach we knew that the four-wheel drive wasn't working well. We figured that "some-wheel drive" up front was better than nothing. Actually, even though the road was little more than a narrow track consisting of two ruts in the sand, the way was really not bad. The thick scrub brush on either side grew right up to a curb formed by sand thrown up from the ruts. If we met anyone, we would be in a standoff. Someone would have to back up a long way.

The change of scenery was nice, though. We actually saw a few real trees—a few trees, yes, but no settlements of any kind. What was shown on the map as a little town turned out to be just a few houses clustered together. We weren't sure whether we had arrived. What we saw really wasn't enough to be considered a community, so we turned right and followed the "road" along the ocean. We still didn't find towns—not even little settlements. I wondered what we would do if we had problems here. Praise God, we didn't. We had gone 30 or 40 kilometers when the trail just sort of petered out at a bar nestled in a little copse of trees on a deserted beach that was being bashed by waves.

Brazilians love their bars. Every tiny little spot in the road has a bar. However, a *bar* is not the noisy, crowded, smoke-filled place you may picture in your mind when you hear that word; the *bar* is as much a gathering place as anything else. When we arrived, this particular bar contained only a couple of men enjoying a beer. We approached the young server and asked her where the road went. We were hoping we wouldn't have to backtrack. Driving here had been OK, but once was enough. Besides, we hadn't seen any towns. The trip would be wasted.

"The road is right across the way," she said as she pointed to the river inlet that curved around in front of the bar.

We looked, but we didn't see a road—not even a trail of a road such as the one on which we had been following for the last couple of hours. I couldn't even discern a place at which the grass was mashed down.

Seeing our puzzled expressions she explained, "You cross on a *balsa*. The boat will be here in a few minutes."

Balsa! Another *balsa!* After our experience of the day before, we weren't about to let someone talk us into something risky today! Today we were on (relatively) solid ground. Even if we had to backtrack, today we wanted to stay on firm footing. Today the truck would still move on its own.

However, on closer inspection, we could see a ramp of sorts to load cars. We resigned ourselves to wait to see what this *balsa* was like. That would not involve driving down the beach. We were keeping our options open.

We went into the bar and took a seat near the railing that served as a wall. The server asked whether we would like something to drink—maybe a beer. Now, Baptist missionaries don't drink alcoholic beverages, but I wondered whether at this point a beer might brighten my outlook. Instead we ordered a couple of soft drinks. The people at the bar assured us that once we crossed the water, we could drive right on down to the town we were trying to find.

The place was relaxing and peaceful. I could see why folks would enjoy gathering here to pass the time of day. Waiting for the *balsa* turned out to be an enjoyable break. As we waited we chatted. Hearing someone speaking English always causes a stir among Brazilians. The men near us heard us talking. Their curiosity was aroused. Soon we were having a stilted conversation with them.

After half an hour or so, the *balsa*, such as the craft was, appeared. The boat was a tiny thing—just large enough for our truck. Even though the motor looked like a weedeater, at least the thing had a motor. We had been on one other *balsa* as small as this one, but that one didn't even have a motor. We had been poled across the river. We opted to cross the river.

The charge to cross the water was R$10. On the other side the road was blocked by a chain. Van looked at the *balsa* pilot, who sourly told us that we had to pay R$2 if we wanted him to lower the chain. *What were we to do?* Ripped off again! Van grudgingly forked over the additional R$2.

The road on this side of the water looked exactly like the one we had left behind. I thought of the trails through the woods back home where I loved to ride horses. I wished I had a horse right then. This place would have been a great place to ride.

The trail gradually turned into a road. Then the road got better and better. We began to see signs of civilization. Soon the road was lined with pastures full of cattle. We saw an occasional house. After we had driven about another hour, we got to a closed gate. On the gate was a sign that was facing the other direction. *Oh great*, I thought. I figured we would have to pay another toll to pass through, but when we stopped, a man who emerged from a guard shack on the other side of the gate proceeded to open the gate for us. Without a comment he waved us through. The road became a street that was the main drag of the town for which we were headed. We had arrived. Curious, I looked back to read the sign on the gate. "Private Property! Authorized personnel only!" the sign proclaimed in bold letters. Guess we were authorized.

Chapter 14

Do You Know the Way to Granja?

As we traveled farther west from Fortaleza, we found that more and more of the oceanfront was covered with the vast sand dunes. Only a few large towns are in that part of the country. Still, the map showed small communities throughout the area; we thought we needed to explore as many of them as we could.

We went to Amontada, situated about 50 kilometers inland, and for two days worked from that town toward the beach. Those were two frustrating days. We were determined to be as thorough as possible by going to every village we could, but we often encountered areas that were impassable. The road would just end abruptly or would lead to an empty beach. Many times we crossed little inches-deep streams of water that straggled across the sand. On one occasion we were going down one of the roads when we decided that no one lived in the area, so going farther was pointless. We had just crossed a little trickle of water. Van made a u-turn and started into the water about three feet from the place at which we had just crossed. In the blink of an eye the whole front end of the truck was under water! This puddle that had looked just like so many others was very different. This stream was very deep. Van stomped on the accelerator. We blasted on through, but we were thoroughly shaken. We definitely had not expected that we were approaching that situation! Van hopped out of the truck to inspect the damage. Fearing the worst—a cracked block—he raised the hood. Water still ran off the various hoses and paraphernalia, but Van didn't think anything major had been damaged. I don't know what we would have done if we had found a problem. We were miles from anywhere. We couldn't even see a house. All we could see was sand sweeping away to the ocean a mile or so in the distance. The place was beautiful but not a good place to break down. We wouldn't find a *guincho* or a mechanic anywhere around here. I didn't see any friendly, helpful, Sandro-type taxi drivers either. Thankfully we were in the truck I had nicknamed *Little Champ*. This truck, like all our cars, had had some problems, but this one never had left us on the side of the road. We weren't let down this time either. Little Champ cranked up like a true champ; we took off. We noticed a few little glitches right at first: the brakes acted weird; a light on the instrument panel kept turning on. For a few minutes things were tense, but once things had time to dry out, we were fine. We realized how God was taking care of us. We could have been beached for days. The walk back to civilization would have been a long, long one. The whole incident left us shaky, so we quit for the day and went back to the hotel.

We didn't locate any Baptist churches here, but we were very happy to see several along the way when we continued west. The town of Acaraú, right on the coast, had a large Baptist church right downtown. We passed through Acaraú and then set our sights on Jericoacoara.

Jericoacoara is one of those Brazilian names that originated from an indigenous language. I don't know what the word means. Thankfully, even the Brazilians have shortened the name to *Jeri*. Jeri is a popular tourist destination for those people who want to see something other than the mega-city beaches and Carnaval. In Jeri one found the eco-tourists like the ones we had glimpsed in our travels in Bahia as well the more adventuresome folks.

The residents of Jeri want to keep the place unspoiled.

When electricity arrived in Jeri, the residents insisted that the wires be buried so that the view would not be polluted with poles and hanging lines.

We slipped down the coastal road easing along from one little village to another. We had a delicious lunch on the beach in Preá while we watched kite-surfers. (Not everything about this job was bad.) After we left Preá, we crossed the dunes of the Jericoacoara National Park and arrived at the town. This time we had followed a trail right on the oceanfront, so getting lost had not been an issue. As we expected Jeri was a bigger town than the type we were looking for but was a neat place to visit. Finding a decent place to stay at a reasonable price was easy here.

Getting out of Jeri the next morning was not as easy as getting to the town had been. We were going to Gijoca de Jericoacoara. This town is on one of the main roads in the area. Sensible people go to Gijoca and hire a guide to go across the dunes to Jeri proper. The map book clearly showed Highway 85 continuing west from Gijoca to Granja. What we wanted to do was to go directly inland across the dunes. This time we saw signs giving directions, but finding the roads on the map in the sand-covered ground in front of us proved to be too difficult. We weren't eager to get stuck (we had that T-shirt), so eventually we backtracked to the highway.

By choosing that tactic, getting to Gijoca was easy. However, once we got to town, we could not find the highway leading to Granja. We weren't ashamed to ask directions. We did our best to follow the ones we got, but once we got to the edge of town, road signs vanished. We went down the roller-coaster road that we were told would lead to Highway 85, but we did not find the turnoff. Convinced that we must have missed the road somehow, we turned around to try again. We retraced our steps all the way back to Gijoca. We asked for directions at the same gas station. The man assured us that the turn to the highway was on the road we had just driven down. Undaunted we struck out again. When for the third time we passed the man with the cows, we stopped to make his acquaintance. Actually, we thought maybe he knew where the highway was.

"Oh, sure," he said. "Just go straight down to the big building on the left and turn. That road will take you to Granja!" He gave us a big old Brazilian grin that encouraged us. His directions sounded easy enough.

The "big" building was a run-down, two-story house, but the place had to be the one about which he spoke, because this building was the biggest one around. A road ran next to the building, so we turned on it. The road didn't look as though it was a highway. This road looked as though it was a driveway. However, we had learned that in Brazil appearances can be deceptive—sometimes, very deceptive. At least the sun wasn't about to go down and the gas tank was three-quarters full. We offered a prayer pleading for guidance and then went. Just as with so many other roads we had traveled, this one seemed to be dwindling away. Any moment we expected the road to end at a house or a waterway or something, but we kept going. We would stop when we got to the end. Eventually the road began to get better. When we got to Parazinho, we knew we would be OK. Parazinho was on the map; better yet, Parazinho was on the road to Granja. From Parazinho to Granja was just a little way; when we got to Granja, the sun still was shining. That had been tricky. Obviously Highway 85 was a work in progress.

Granja was not much of a town, so we drove another 30 kilometers on a black-topped road to Camocim to spend the night. Camocim had a *pousada*. Camocim had a nice park and a dock lined with fishing boats. Camocim had a neat French restaurant. For dessert we had Crème Brulee. We slept well in Camocim. The next morning we stepped over a big iguana on our stoop as we started back again. After all the trouble we had gone through to get here, now we had to go back to Fortaleza. The SUV that had broken down with us in Bahia and was repaired in Brasilia was supposed to be delivered any day. We had to be at home to receive the truck.

Keeping a vehicle in running condition seemed to be a constant issue with us. The truck we had gotten in Recife now was having issues with the front end, the air-conditioning, and the four-wheel drive. Whenever we were in Fortaleza, we constantly were taking the vehicle to the shop. The folks at the mechanic's shop knew the Americans well. We had become friends. However, now that we had we had gotten this truck in good running condition, we would swap this one for the SUV that was being released from its hospital stay in Brasilia. The SUV had been in Brasilia for six months. We were expecting that truck to be in top shape. We were excited about that. At the same time we were sort of sad to say goodbye to Little Champ. We had demanded a lot of that truck. Despite all the problems the truck had served us well.

When we got back to Fortaleza, we still had to wait several days for the SUV. The day it arrived was exciting. We were impressed with what we saw. The SUV now had a big wench on the front. The four-wheel drive was supposed to be in good shape. Less impressive was the condition of the truck. The thing was filthy. We wondered how many days the truck had been on the car hauler. We wanted to get the truck cleaned right away.

In the U.S. when you take a car to the car wash, the job usually takes half an hour or so. In Brazil you'd better take a good book and expect to wait at least two hours. We took the SUV to our favorite car wash in Fortaleza. This car wash was near Beira Mar Hotel. Taking the car to that place meant we could kill time wandering around the shops and restaurants and watching people while we waited. When we returned, the SUV was sparkling. How nice to have good-looking, dependable vehicle for a change. Now we were equipped for those difficult roads. We were ready for any situation. Or so we thought.

Chapter 15

Working in the Delta

Although most of our days were spent on the road, sometimes we had the opportunity to combine business and pleasure. Such was the case when we were working near the border of Piauí. Our colleagues, Vic and Sharon, who had been in Brazil many years, live in Parnaíba, Piauí, a big town near the coast. They work along the coast as well as on some of the nearby islands. At the missions's annual meeting we had had the opportunity to get to know this couple. They invited us to drop in for a visit when we got to their neck of the woods. When we visited them, they had been working in the coastal area of Piauí for about seven years. They had helped establish churches on some nearby islands in the area known as *The Delta* and were eager to show them to us. They also wanted to go to some areas where they wanted to start a Baptist church.

On our first day with them, Vic, an avid fisherman, hired a boat to take us to the island of Caiçara. The day, like so many days on the northern coast of Brazil, was gorgeous. We were armed with sunscreen and hats as we loaded into the small speed boat for our trip. Sharon said the trip would take about 45 minutes in the fast boat that we were taking that day. We jolted over the waves with the wind whipping our faces. The feeling was wonderful. When we got to the island, we walked about half a mile to the house of the young women who worked in the church and school. The time was about 10 in the morning. When we arrived, the young women were frying fish for us; the cat who lingered nearby seemed to think this was a great idea. The house, connected to the school and the church, was fairly new. As with most Brazilian homes this one was

117

very clean. When I looked out the window I didn't see any traffic, because the island doesn't have roads or cars. In this isolated place everyone walks or travels by boat. In fact, when I looked out the window, I didn't see much besides sand, water, and a few palm trees. The place was very quiet, even though several people were walking around doing this and that. We had a fish snack that we shared with the cat. Then we were given a tour. The little school was full of children up to about the age of 7 or 8. One little girl was hearing-impaired. She was a little frightened by our visit. I don't think she ever had seen people like us, but we convinced her to pose with the rest of the kids for pictures. Digital cameras are so nice because we could show the children their pictures immediately. They were tickled to see themselves in our camera.

After we visited the school, we went over to see the church. Unlike some of the nooks where we'd seen Baptists meet, the church was a nice, solid building. Before we headed back to the boat to go to another village, I took several photos. The village to which we were going had no Baptist work.

After a short boat ride, we stopped on a strip of empty beach. Vic took off walking up a path that led inland. We all followed him. The time by now was about 11 in the morning. At this time of day on the north coast of Brazil the temperature is very hot. The sun is merciless. During this part of the day the local people usually stay inside their houses. However, a few men were loitering beneath a thatch-roofed shed we passed. Vic stopped to say *hello*. The men were curious as to why we were out walking in the heat of the day, but with a laugh they declined Vic's offer to join us.

The path led through scrubby brush. As we walked, we passed only an occasional hut. The sand was so hot that if our feet slid off the sides of our flip-flops, they were almost blistered. After 10 minutes or so we began to see a few more houses. I got glimpses of the people peeking out at us from the inside. I imagined they were probably thinking that we were highly educated North Americans who didn't have enough sense to stay out of the midday sun!

We walked and walked with Vic as our fearless leader. I was glad we had protection against the brutal sun. Finally Sharon decided she had had enough.

"Vic," she yelled, "how much farther are you going to go?"

"I want to get to the little village just on up the trail," he yelled back.

Sharon relented. We kept going, but, when after another 10 or 15 minutes we still hadn't gone the "little way" to the village, Sharon called out that she was done. She told Vic that if he wanted to keep going, that was OK with her, but she was going to wait right here in the shade of the *cajueira* (cashew tree) until he returned. This time Vic relented, but I could tell he was a little disappointed as he gazed wistfully down the trail. We all took a break in the shade before we started back.

Along the way we had passed a well at which the people got their "fresh" water. The well was just a hole slanted into the ground. Some steps carved into one side allowed a person to ease down and fill his vessel. The water didn't look suitable for livestock, let alone people. This was the only place in all of our travels around Brazil that I saw such a well. I asked whether this was their only source of fresh water. Vic said he thought so. The steps were worn, so the well obviously was used a lot.

On our way back to the boat, we again passed the men at the hut. As we went by, they grinned at us as if to say, "We told you so." We grinned back. I guess that now had become our little inside joke.

The weather was very hot, but the thing that struck me as unusual, being a girl from the Deep South, was that as soon as we stepped out of the direct sun, everything was fine. This was

119

not like the hot, humid summer days to which I was accustomed in Arkansas and Louisiana. I guess the strong sea breezes made the difference. Still, the weather was hot. As we zipped over the water, I was glad we were in the boat with the wind in our faces. We passed through some inlets with mangroves growing on either side. The waves were rough; the tide was coming in. Going across the waves was like riding a bucking horse. Every time we crashed down on the surface, we got shaken all the way through. Sharon told me that tomorrow we would go to some other villages on the islands, but we would take the slow boat. The bigger boat would be smoother. That was good news to me.

Our last stop on the way in was to eat. After eating we went straight back to Tutus, where we had rented the boat. Van and I helped unload the boat. While we took the stuff to the truck, Vic settled up with the boat "captain." When he joined us at the truck, he told us we were going to give a ride to a young woman and her baby son. I asked Vic how he had known she needed a ride. His reply? *She asked me.* That explained that.

The truck already was full, because one of the young women from Caiçara was going back to Parnaíba with us, so the woman and her baby crawled into the back. I was scared to death thinking of that little tyke riding in the back, so I offered to hold him in my lap up front. (I needed a baby fix anyway, since I hadn't seen my grandbabies in several months.) He seemed happy among all these strangers; he was quite an agreeable child.

Driving in Brazil always is an experience; driving there after dark can be a little daunting even in a less-populated area. On our short journey back to Parnaíba, we had several unsettling episodes. I was glad the baby was in the cab of the truck. As we pulled in to town, the woman asked Vic to stop, so he pulled over at a street corner. The woman got out, thanked us, and retrieved her baby. Then, as we all watched in amazement, she crossed the street and engaged a *moto-taxi* for her and the child. She clambered on board the motorcycle, snuggled junior in between her and the driver, and they were off. Well, we had done what we could.

When we arrived at Vic and Sharon's house, we sat around talking way into the night even though the next day was going to be a busy one. Eventually everyone wandered off to bed.

The next morning bright and early we were back on the road to Tutus. Today we were going to visit some places in which Vic and Sharon were working with Brazilian Baptists. We also would meet the young pastor who was serving at a church on one of the islands. Going out would be no problem, but the tide would go out in the middle of the day. That meant we would have to wait until the water again was deep enough for our boat before we could continue. Vic said we probably would pass the time fishing. *Aww, shuckins!*

The slow boat definitely was slower but a lot more comfortable. The boat had a roof and wooden seats along the sides and rear. A hammock was suspended from the uprights on the side. Vic clambered into the hammock to demonstrate the proper Brazilian way to use one. He did such a good job that soon he was snoring.

We eased along near the bank to get an up-close look at the mangroves growing at the water's edge before we went out into the open water. This day we had a dock on which to disembark when we reached our destination instead of just a small beach, but we still had to walk a long way on sand paths into the village.

The young pastor was excited about the church's new building. He showed us the large, multi-purpose building that was almost finished. Finding so much Baptist work in such an out-of-the-way place was rewarding. I was thankful that Vic and Sharon were willing to be used by God here.

After our tour, we loaded back into the boat and headed to a restaurant for lunch. The place was just a crude hut set at the end of a wooden pier. This restaurant probably was the only eatery for miles around. We were surprised to run into a small group of English-speaking Europeans. We spent some time talking to them.

For lunch we ordered fish. At a seaside café fish usually is a good choice, but I think they actually had to catch the fish first. From the time we ordered until we boarded the boat again was more than two hours, but the food and the company were good. We all enjoyed our lunch. Vic cleaned up all the scraps. Back on the boat we had gone only a little way before, sure enough, we had to stop because the tide was out. The water was too low for us to cross. Vic dragged out all the fishing gear. Everyone, including the captain and his wife, fished—everyone, that is, except me. Vic climbed up on top of the roof of the boat. Every now and then he'd holler out that he'd caught a little fish. No one else was catching anything. Then all of a sudden Van jumped.

"I've got one! A big one!" he exclaimed.

The captain hurried to help Van pull the fish in.

"*È grande! È grande!*" he kept repeating. (It's big! It's big!)

Sure enough, the fish was big. When the captain grabbed the line with his hand, the big fish pulled back with so much strength, the line cut the captain's hand, but he hung on anyway. He wasn't going to let that big boy get away! By that time Vic had arrived to lend a hand. In a short time the fish was in the boat. Van was grinning from ear to ear. Vic was as excited as if he had been the one to snag the whopper. The fish was a grouper that weighed about 12 pounds. We all were laughing and talking. Suddenly I remembered something else. The day was Van's birthday! What a neat gift!

Van's landing of that big fish encouraged everyone to keep fishing. The captain kept saying he was going to get that one's papa, but the fish must have been an orphan, because *that one* was the only fish we caught the rest of the day. Finally the tide rose enough to weigh anchor and go home. As the light slowly drained from the sky, the old boat puttered along. When we pulled into the dock, the sun was long gone. We were four tired, happy people. We decided that until our next visit we would leave the prize catch with Vic. Then we would have a fish feast.

The two days with Vic and Sharon had been productive and fun. We had learned a lot about the Delta area and the Baptist work being done in that part of the country. We had had a marvelous experience in traveling to the islands. Good friendships had been forged.

Chapter 16

Going to Barreirinhas

"This has to be the road," I said as Van slowed up so we could look down the way. As we had passed by, he had seen this road, so we had backtracked to take a closer look. The day before we had crossed over into the Brazilian state of Maranhão and driven down to the coastal city of Tutoias. In Tutoias we had found the sand track that served as a road on over to the village of Paulino Neves. While we were trying to find our way out of Paulino Neves, we had discovered that the four-wheel drive on the SUV we had just gotten back from an overhaul was not working.

We had driven into the town, which had a boulevard in the center. One side the street was only partially cobblestoned, but we weren't concerned when we dipped off the end into the sand. We already had driven miles in sand that looked just like this little patch. Besides, we had four-wheel drive.

As soon as we left the cobblestones, we realized that this sand was not like the sand on which we had been driving because, much to our consternation, even though the four-wheel drive was supposed to be engaged, we found ourselves stuck just as quickly as we had been the day on the beach. Besides being frustrating the situation also was very embarrassing. Here two *gringos* from who-knew-where and who thought they were so smart now were stuck in the middle of a town with an interested audience watching closely. Since we were stuck, we couldn't do anything but just sit in the road and look really stupid. A Bandeirante truck approaching us from the other direction stopped when the driver saw us. That thing could go just about anywhere. The driver and his "co-pilot"

124

were as amused as the other onlookers were, but they looked as though they'd be willing to help. Van raised his hands in the universal signal of helplessness. Sure enough, the guys pulled over. I guess they were a little puzzled about why we weren't using the honking big wench on the front of our truck to pull us out. We didn't explain to them that someone had stolen the control to the wench while the truck was in the shop having major repairs done—repairs that should have included the four-wheel drive. They hooked a rope to the rear bumper; in no time we were back on solid ground. After we used our best Portuguese to express our sincerest thanks, we decided to get something to eat. At a time such as this, food always helps. We found a good little restaurant with a friendly owner and had a lunch of plain old Country food. We told the restaurant owner that we were trying to go through to Barreirinhas. He told us that the road west of town was much worse than the one from Tutoias. That statement decided for us. Obviously the four-wheel drive on the truck was not working. We would go back to Tutoias. Then we would find the road we had seen on the map from the highway into Barreirinhas. We figured that way would be much better. Now we were on the highway looking for said road.

The road at which we were looking right now was a wide, well-maintained one with a solid gravel surface. According to the map, from where we sat to Barreirinhas was about 80 kilometers.

We hadn't gone far before the road became the roughest, wash-boardiest road on which we'd ever traveled. That is saying a lot, because Arkansas has lots of rough roads. Surely we wouldn't have to drive 80 kilometers on a road like this. While we were jolting along discussing the condition of the road, we passed a man just moseying along on a tractor.

"Let's ask him," I suggested.

So Van pulled over and shouted, "Is this the way to Barreirinhas?" By now we were getting good at asking that sort of question.

The tractor driver couldn't hear us, so he stopped and got out. He was a great big, un-Brazilian-looking guy named Daltro. Even though he didn't look Brazilian, he had the typical Brazilian helpful attitude. He looked at our map and finally figured out what we wanted to know.

"*Hmm*," he said "Yes. I think this road goes to Barreirinhas, but I don't know what the way is like. I've never been to the town on this road."

That should have given us a clue. Instead we thanked him and started off again. After a bit the road got smoother. We began to take in the scenery and noted the thatched-roof houses and farms we passed. Today things seemed to be going better, but that was only an illusion.

To our dismay, when we had driven about 40 kilometers, the road began to get worse again. This time the problem was not the rub-board bumpiness. Now the road began to get narrower and sandier. This was not good, but we had driven so far now that turning back didn't seem like a good option. For the time being we were OK. The farther we drove, the more the road continued to deteriorate. Now we were driving in the sand. Van didn't dare stop or even slow down. We didn't want to get stuck out here. Stopping would have meant sticking.

As usual on these back roads, we happened onto lots of crossroads that weren't shown on the map. When we would encounter one, we would just follow our noses and pray for the best. Once, when we had a place solid enough to stop for a second, we checked our GPS just to see whether we at least still were headed toward the ocean. Imagine our distress when even the GPS didn't know where we were. When that happens, you know you're in trouble.

Knowing what to do in a situation like this is so difficult. We already were so committed. Besides, we shouldn't have far to go now, right? Maybe we should have just been committed to a funny farm! Turning around might have been wiser, but I'm not sure we could have found our way back anyway. Whatever, we kept going. At last we saw a sign of civilization: a lumber mill. We pulled in and told the people where we wanted to go.

"Just a minute," we were told. "We have a boy working here who lives in that town. He can show you the way."

We were filled with relief. We just knew that this trying trip was nearing an end.

Soon a young man walked out and climbed in our back seat. He was very polite but very quiet. His comments were mainly restricted to, "Turn here", or, "Go straight ahead." We could understand those commands.

Although the narrow road was not as sandy here, the lane still was getting narrower and narrower. On both sides were steep earthen banks as if the thing had been chiseled out of the earth. I was convinced that soon we were going to be scraping the walls. We couldn't turn back now even if we tried. I could imagine us getting wedged in to the point that we couldn't even open the door, but I just held my breath and hung on to the idea that we couldn't have much farther to go. Our predicament was very nerve-wracking.

Then, just when I didn't think things could get worse, they did. We arrived at a place in which the road became filled with huge ruts. On the right side the tiny strip of road had enough room for the tires, but on the left was a ledge just inches wide that climbed up the side of the embankment. To get beyond that stretch of the road we would have to straddle an abyss. If we fell off, we would be stuck in a manner that would make the beach episode look like a picnic. Van masterfully drove the left-hand wheels up the tiny ledge. I couldn't look. If we slipped off, we would be in deep trouble—literally and figuratively. But we didn't fall. We passed the challenging spot and reached the somewhat-wider road beyond. Things were better, but that wasn't saying a lot. Things didn't have to be very good to be better.

By now we both had our doubts about the validity of our guide. He seemed to be directing us away from the place we wanted to go, but not even our GPS knew for sure. Finally we happened onto a little settlement. Our new friend told us how to get to his house. When we arrived, he got out, thanked us, and started walking away.

"Wait! Wait!" we cried. "Is this Barreirinhas?"

"*Não, não,*" he replied with a grin. "*É direta*" (No, no. It's straight ahead), he indicated with a wave of his hand.

"How far?" we asked. We expected him to say just two or three more kilometers.

His grin widened. "About 70 kilometers," he said as he walked away. So much for helpful Brazilians.

We looked at each other. Seventy more kilometers? How could that be? The whole trip was supposed to be only about 80 kilometers. We already had been traveling for hours. We were beginning to feel a little desperate. The time was getting late. We were out in the middle of nowhere without an idea of how to get to somewhere. The good news was that at the time, we were blessedly ignorant of the fact that our adventure was far from over.

We drove far enough to be out of the young man's sight. Then we stopped to talk this over between ourselves and with God. I think God was all that kept me from breaking down into great big sobs. We had no realistic choice other than to continue, but which way were we to go? Remember in *The Wizard of Oz* when Dorothy reaches a crossroad? She sees that helpful scarecrow who gives her directions to the Emerald City. We could have used a scarecrow at this point—even a confused one. A GPS would have been great, too. I don't know what the problem was with ours. I guess we were really, really lost. All we had was our sense of direction and the firm belief that we were in God's hands. He knew exactly where we were.

At least we were in a little community. The people had to have some way to get in and out of here. We struck off in the most promising-looking direction. That road wound through the village. From various nooks and crannies the local people watched us curiously and discreetly as we passed their houses. In these parts strangers obviously were rare. Then we ran into a water crossing. This presented a big, big problem. The water really didn't look too deep, but we already had had unpleasant experiences as we crossed seemingly innocent puddles. Plus, we knew our four-wheel drive was not dependable.

What to do, what to do? Suppose we drive off into that water and drop to the bottom as though we were rocks. *Hmm.* First, we would be utterly humiliated in front of the locals. Then we would have the immediate problem of how we were going to get the truck out of the hole. (No Bandeirantes were in this remote place. We had only a useless wench on the truck.) After that we'd have to deal with the probability of major engine damage. Then we would have to figure out how to get home. Lastly we'd have to explain to Ed just exactly how we ended up drowning our truck in the boonies of Brazil. None of this was appealing (especially the explaining-to-Ed part.) Surely we could find a way around this spot. We turned around to look for another route. As we passed a house on a curve, we saw a woman with her hair wrapped in a towel; she looked as though she had just stepped out of the shower. She walked out to the edge of the road and flagged us down. She had seen us going back and forth. Without asking she knew that we were looking for a way out of here. She knew how to get us out.

"You need to go back the way you were going," she said as she pointed toward the water crossing.

"Are you sure?" Van asked. "Can you drive through that water?"

"Yes, I'm sure. Just drive straight through," she said with a smile.

We were skeptical. Was she being helpful, or did she just relish the idea of seeing us sink? We doubted that she ever had driven a car anywhere, let alone through that pool.

While we pondered, she nodded her head encouragingly. We looked at each other.

"What other choice do we have?" Van asked.

"None, I guess. Oh, dear Lord, please get us through this water," I prayed. Van agreed.

So, we turned around again. We arrived at the edge of the water and stopped. We sat and stared at the huge puddle as though we were kids trying to gather enough courage to jump off the high board at the swimming pool. Finally Van took a deep breath and charged into the water. Down we went. The water splashed up over the windshield. We went up the other side. We almost reached the top. The engine groaned and struggled. The tires spun. The onlookers grinned bigger. I thought my heart was going to stop. Van rammed his foot down on the accelerator; with a final lunge we lurched out of the water. The sensation was almost as if we had willed ourselves to the other side. For several minutes we stopped to get control of our trembling selves. We just sat and thanked God for bringing us safely across. When we regained enough strength to continue, we realized that we still didn't have a real road under us. We still had no plan. We still were lost.

We had only one direction we could go, so we drove that way. Soon we encountered a bunch of men working in the path. To the right was what seemed to be the beginnings of a new road. To the left was a rocky incline that perhaps a sure-footed goat might traverse. Van lowered the window. He told the man closest to him where we were trying to go. With his hand the man waved to the left and said the very familiar words: "*È direta!*" (It's straight ahead.)

Straight ahead? Straight ahead? You couldn't go straight anywhere around here. This truck was not about to try going up that hill to the left!

Van pointed incredulously to the hill and asked, "That way?"

"Oh, no, no," the man replied. "Around that way," he said as he pointed to the right.

What a relief! We were so happy to follow the cow path to the right, we took off without even thanking the man.

The path gradually got better. Once again we were lulled into believing that at last we were on the right track. Things really seemed to be looking up when the path turned into a real road. Before long we found ourselves following one of the Bandeirante trucks known in the area as *pau de arara* (parrot perches). Van and I simply called them "people-movers". They basically are high-clearance pick-up trucks with benches—the perches—lining the bed and a cover over the top. In this part of Brazil these trucks serve as buses, because they represent a very dependable way to get around in this sand-covered land.

Seeing the people-mover encouraged us. The people-mover must be taking people somewhere, right? We followed the people-mover until the truck stopped to unload people. We passed the truck then, but we were confident that this road, which now was very good, surely led into town. We cruised along for several kilometers before the road suddenly made a sharp, left-hand turn and ended at a locked gate.

OK, now what? We couldn't go forward. We already knew what was behind us. I had seen no other roads. We were on the brink of desperation and trying to regroup when, lo and behold, we saw the people-mover approaching! That truck had to be going to go through the gate. Now we'd find out what to do. When the driver got out to open the gate, I ran over to him. I asked him whether we had to go through that gate to get to town. He gave me a perplexed look. I thought his confusion was caused by more than just my Portuguese.

"Why, no," he replied, "this is private property. Town is back that way." He pointed in the direction we had just traveled.

My mouth dropped open. I couldn't speak in English, let alone Portuguese. He obviously wanted to help me, but all he could do—in his kindest voice—was to tell me to backtrack.

Finally I managed to say, "'*Ta bom. 'Ta bom.*" (OK, OK). Then in a daze I walked back to the truck. I was trying to absorb this new information. Backtracking would lead nowhere. I knew that. Ahead was forbidden territory.

When I reported this news to Van, at first he was as confused as I was. Then he started thinking. In times such as these I gain insight into the function of a marriage. While I didn't know what to do other than to cry, my husband acted more resourcefully. In his mind he began to backtrack until he remembered we had passed a trail that led off to left. I had been so intent on following the people-mover and so convinced that our problems were behind us that I hadn't even seen the road. Clearly God paired us because Van sees those things and I don't. (I have other admirable qualities!) Marriage partners usually complement each other like that.

Anyway, we headed back as we looked for the little road Van had remembered. Sure enough, we found the road. By now the hour was really getting late. The prospects for finding lodging for the night were looking dim. We discussed the very real possibility of sleeping in the truck. I was more frightened than I had ever been in all our travels. Crying still seemed as though it was a viable option to me. But I didn't cry.

Van just kept driving. Eventually the road did get better, but now we were skeptical. That had happened before; it hadn't meant a thing. This time, though, the road kept getting better and wider and more solid. Then we began to meet traffic. That's always a good sign—especially when the traffic consists of cars and trucks and not donkeys and ox carts or people-movers! The road became a dual road of sorts. Appearances were that someday, someone might try to blacktop this road. As we tried to pick the best sections of the road, we wove from lane to lane like all the other vehicles were doing. Then we fell in behind another people-mover. Its driver seemed to know the road, so we went where that truck went.

The road that seemed so wonderful to us at the time was good only by comparison with the one on which we had traveled most of the day. This good road still was a dirt road and was full of undulations, holes, and ruts. But, hey, we weren't going to complain. We hoped we finally were heading toward civilization. However, until we arrived, I wouldn't believe we actually were going somewhere!

When I began to fret about what we would find at the end of our journey, Van assured me that everything would be OK. How interesting that my husband, not the most optimistic of people, suddenly became so confident that things would be OK in circumstances such as the ones in which we found ourselves that day. I still was worried because the sun was low in the sky and we still were wandering around in unfamiliar territory. Our conversation dried up. We traveled along in silence; both of us were lost in our own thoughts.

At last I saw what I thought was a water tank on top of a house. My heart leapt. Van saw the tank, too. I think he began to drive a little faster. About a kilometer ahead the road made a little bend and ended at a blacktop highway. Van slammed on the brakes and screeched to a halt. In awe we sat and stared at the asphalt road. Now I felt like crying tears of joy. Actually I

133

thought about jumping out of the truck, running over, and kissing the pavement the way people in old movies did when their ships at sea reached land.

"Praise God! Praise God!" Van sighed. I could tell he was really moved, too. "Look," he continued, "the sun is still shining."

"Well, let's go see if we can find a *pousada*."

With renewed energy we took off again. Right away we saw a sign that told us that Barreirinhas was about five kilometers ahead. I thought again of the Emerald City. I hoped we'd find the wizard, because our quest was not over yet.

The sign had been accurate. Barreirinhas was a short distance up the road. After chasing after the town all day I was glad that the place was pretty big. Finding a place to stay also was easy. We stopped at a fancy *pousada,* but after we heard the price, we decided to look elsewhere. The clerk told us about another place. She said that *pousada* was more economical and might be just what we wanted. She was exactly right. The other place was perfect.

Never had two people been more grateful to settle into a hotel room. To us the humble lodging could have been the Ritz. This had been a challenging day, but by the grace of God and with His guidance and mercy we had reached our goal. Tomorrow was another day. Tomorrow we would start over. Tonight we were going to rest.

Chapter 17

Up the River in a Boat

Barreirinhas. After a very difficult, challenging day we finally had reached our destination. The place wasn't The Land of Oz, but the town wasn't bad. We found a good place to stay and collapsed into bed. The next morning the first order of business was to see whether we really could get the four-wheel drive on the SUV repaired. We wanted to get some work done without having to go into São Luis or, worse yet, back to Fortaleza to get the truck fixed.

We talked to Enzo, the owner of the *pousada*, about our problem. To help us he lined up a local man named Raimundo. Raimundo was a jack-of-all-trades-type fellow who was eager to be of assistance to these wandering Americans. We all hopped into the truck; then Raimundo directed us to the best mechanic in town—at least that's how we later would think of him, because he actually was able to get the four-wheel drive working again. Having got that done Raimundo wanted to give us a tour. He directed us to his home on a small *sitio* (a little farm) with a few chickens and fruit trees. He was very proud of his little farm. He took us around and showed us each plant and pointed out every animal. He was particularly proud of his well. Since Barreirinhas is close to the ocean, having a fresh-water well is a prize. His well, he said, was great. To prove this he took the length of plugged PVC pipe used as a bucket and drew some water. Then he poured some into the plastic cup that sat on the edge of the well and offered the water to us. We had been taught that to refuse this kind of hospitality would be a real slap in the face to the person making the effort, so we each took a sip from the cup. The water was really good. We just didn't think about what else may have been in the cup. Missionaries all know the prayer, "Lord, I'll put it down. You please keep it down." Raimundo could tell we were country people and enjoyed seeing the animals. He told us that if we wanted, we could buy some nearby property that was for sale. We politely declined.

Anyone who meets me quickly learns that I am crazy about horses. Raimundo was no different. He realized that seeing a horse up close and personal would lift my spirits, so he took us to see one at his father-in-law's house. Unfortunately, the horse was not nearly as interested in meeting me as I was in meeting him. Seeing him did help my feelings, though. Someone once said, "There's something about the outside of a horse that is good for the inside of a (wo)man."

We explained to Raimundo that we needed to go to some villages situated right on the coast. The villages were not accessible by road—at least, not by any roads we were eager to explore. We needed a boat. We asked whether he could arrange for someone to take us out to the towns the next day. He said that he could. He told us that later that evening he would send the man over to the *pousada*. After we made those arrangements, we returned Raimundo to his house. Then we went out to eat.

The day had been such an improvement over the one before. In Barreirinhas we found a really good, reasonably priced *churrascaria* (*shoo-hahs-cah-RE-ah*). A *churrasco* is a Brazilian barbecue; the *churrascaria* is the place in which they cook the *churrasco*. The meat is roasted on skewers over an open fire. In some *churrascarias* they bring to your table skewers loaded with meat. You select the type of meat you want; the server slices off as much as you request. Servers go from table to table with all types of meat. If they don't give you very much, you don't have to worry. They'll be back! Usually the problem is trying to eat what you have before they return. A restaurant with this type of service is called a *chur-rascaria rodizo*. A *rodizo* is like an all-you-can-eat buffet that they bring to you. The *churrascaria* in Barreirinhas was not *rodizo*, but the food was excellent. We were happy to have found such a good place to eat. Slowly the emotional wounds of the agonizing trip were healing.

After we ate, we went "home" and met with the boat captain and his wife. We made plans to set out the next day at 8 a.m.

The captain's wife arrived right on time to show us the way to the boat. The river was about a quarter of a mile behind the *pousada*. The trail led through a small, wooded area. The air was crisp. In the morning light the river was beautiful. Yes, things definitely were looking up.

The boat was a little outboard. Soon we were settled in and on our way. I was happy not to have to worry about directions or to make the correct turns. The salt air in our faces seemed to blow away the concerns of recent days. Our captain was competent. To stay in the channel he swerved from side to side. We just sat back and enjoyed the ride.

Our destination was the village of Atins, but along the way we would be making a couple of other stops. We would go down the river and along the coast to reach Atins in the *Parque Nacional dos Lençois*. That is the Sheets National Park. The park gets its name from the miles and miles of coastland covered with huge sheets of sand. This sand is what made getting stuck in Paulino Neves so easy.

We traveled for an hour or so and then stopped to take a break. The place at which we stopped was built right on the beach to cater to any passing tourists. Basically the spot was a tourist trap. Nothing else was nearby. The shop consisted of a *lanchonete* and a gift shop of sorts. The shopkeepers had a monkey that was more or less a pet. He lived in the jungle, but for a fee he would visit with guests. He was an "if-you've-got-the-bananas, I've-got-the-time" sort of guy. The owner provided us with bananas, so we took advantage of the photo op. The monkey climbed around on our shoulders and enjoyed the bananas. Afterward we felt obligated to buy something, so we picked out a little purse and two bottles of water. Then we were on our way again.

The next stop was Mandacaru. In Mandacaru we had a conversation with a man who was running for councilman. He was really interested in knowing whether we were registered to vote in his little town. That is just like a politician always to be looking for votes. We talked to him a little about the various churches in town, but that subject didn't interest him nearly as much as the election did.

Mandacaru has a lighthouse, so of course we had to climb to the top. During our travels we had seen many lighthouses, but we never had climbed one. We walked the short jaunt over to the lighthouse and then started climbing. Our guide told us that the lighthouse had 300 steps. I silently thanked God for giving me the health to be able to climb them without stressing out. The climb was worth the effort. From the top you could see for miles, uh . . . kilometers. From that vantage point one thing we very easily could tell: we never would have been able to drive to this place. We left the lighthouse and headed on to Atins.

When we pulled up on the beach at Atins, I was sort of wondering why we had stopped. I didn't see a town. However, I didn't say anything; I simply followed our trustworthy leader down the beach to a trail leading inland. Walking in the sand in flip-flops is really good exercise. You get a good workout, especially if you follow a young Brazilian man used to trekking these trails regularly. Walking behind him made me think of following Vic all over the place that day, except this guy walked faster than Vic did.

Atins is a little town that is tucked up in the trees. You had to wonder what ever lured people to live here in the first place. On the trail on the way in we passed a thatch-roofed *pousada*. The place looked fairly new, so I supposed the people were catering to the "eco-tourists", too. Before we went back to the boat, we had another bottle of water and a nice conversation with the young women who worked at the store. After we left Atins, we talked about what we had seen and learned that day. Besides the fact that this visit was beneficial for our research, we had had a great time there. Our job certainly had its draw-backs, but Van and I considered ourselves so blessed to have the opportunity to visit these backwater areas and see these lit-tle-visited parts of the world. We were so richly blessed indeed.

Chapter 18

Stuck Again!

One thing we had learned after our trip to Barreirinhas was that just because a road was shown on the map didn't mean we *really* would find a *real* road in the *real* world.

Today our destination was the town of Santo Amaro do Maranhão. Since we had a newfound respect for those map roads, we took the coward's way out and followed the paved road to the town of Humberto de Campo.

Humberto de Campo is a fairly large town—bigger than the ones for which we were looking. We were happy to find a Baptist church in the city anyway.

After investigating Humberto de Campo, we had to bite the bullet and leave the pavement behind. Now we were looking for the turnoff to Santo Amaro do Maranhão. Santo Amaro is situated right on the coast of Brazil in the Lençóis. This huge national park supposedly has wildlife, but we never saw any.

Once you leave the highway, traveling is difficult. If you don't have four-wheel drive, you had better stay on the pavement. But we had four-wheel drive now; Santo Amaro was one of the places we had to check out. We were loaded for bear! So, even though we knew that the road on the map might not really exist, we were cruising along looking for the turnoff. The book gave some very specific instructions about how to get to Santo Amaro; apparently the town was trying to attract eco-tourists. Several times we went back and forth and zeroed in on the supposed turn like a pendulum slowly reaching a stop. All of a sudden I noticed a sign we had passed at least twice; it directed drivers to a "resort" in Santo Amaro.

To our dismay the road was a narrow, one-way sand track. We had experienced just about as much of those roads as we wanted. This one was just wide enough for a single vehicle. Thick, foreboding underbrush lined both sides. We knew that once we started down this road, we wouldn't be able to turn back. We had been in that position before, so we stopped and considered. At least now the four-wheel drive was fixed . . . hopefully. We decided to pray; leaving the matter in God's hands, we started off. The truck was running well, but out loud Van wondered what we would do if we met anyone. We wouldn't be able to get out of the way. Both of us kept a steady stream of protection prayers going heavenward.

According to the map book Santo Amaro should be 34 kilometers ahead. Without incident we drove merrily along for a long time, but today we were expecting the worst and were prepared for just about anything.

After several kilometers we arrived at an intersection at which our sand track met a wide, solid, gravel road. *Well, shoot! All that stress for nothing.* We could have used that road, provided, of course that we could have found that road! At least now we knew we could go out that way. Now we understood why we hadn't met any cars going out the way we entered, but that was a good thing. At this spot we saw a couple of little stores and a bus stop. Some folks were hanging around. We took advantage of this to ask directions. We were relieved to know that we were going the right direction. Having this better road would make the going easier and less stressful. We breathed a sigh of relief.

Our relief was premature. Not far past the intersection, the road made a little bend to the left, crossed a bridge, and then, lo and behold, we were right back on the same type of road we had just left. So much for the better road! As bad as this one was, however, we considered the road much better than the road to Barreirinhas had been. At least here we saw evidence of civilization. Along the way some houses were scattered. We saw people-movers going both directions. The time was early in the afternoon; except for a few tense moments, we were moving across the sand well. Van was driving skillfully. We thought we might be in Santo Amaro by the middle of the afternoon. Maybe we would have time to find a place to spend the night and to relax a little.

Things seemed to be going well, but that all changed in the blink of an eye—well, actually in the turn of a wheel. We went over a little rise. The road ahead looked the same as we what we had seen for the last 20 or 30 kilometers, but as we headed toward the bottom of the little dip, we suddenly got stuck. I was astounded. So close but so far away! Even though we had four-wheel drive, our SUV wasn't high enough to clear the sand. The back end of the truck was sitting on the sand.

At first we weren't too upset about this turn of events. In a way I guess we had been expecting something such as this to happen. We believed that a people-mover soon would be along to help us. Then we would be back on the road again. We got out and began to use our flip-flops to shovel sand away from the wheels. Really, we did this just to think we were doing something productive. That was a really discouraging endeavor, because the sand collapsed in on the wheels as fast as we could dig. While Van kept digging, I scrounged around for something to put under the wheels. For a while we thought we actually might be able to free the truck, but in the end the sand won. By now we were hot and sweaty and wondering what had happened to all those people-movers.

"How far did the map book say Santo Amaro was from the highway?" Van asked. "We should be nearly to the town."

I leaned into the truck to check the odometer. Sure enough, according to the instrument, we should have only a few more kilometers to go. That was when I became aware of the music.

Around election time in Brazil a popular method of campaigning is to use sound cars. These vehicles mounted with loudspeaker systems go around blasting out the virtues of the various candidates. Sometimes they include catchy little jingles. We had encountered them even in the smallest little backwater communities. Sometimes the sound "car" consisted of a loudspeaker on a bicycle. Sometimes the sound was from a huge truck and trailer similar to the *trio electricos* used at Carnaval celebrations in São Paulo, Salvador, and other places. These big trucks traveled the road loaded with "supporters." We once passed one on a sand trail of a road way out in the middle of nowhere. The sound was so loud that when we passed, our truck vibrated. I didn't consider them "good, good, good vibrations", as the line from the popular song went. I won't tell you what I did think of them. Regardless, right now we could hear the familiar noise; for once the sound truly was music to my ears.

"Let's start walking," my beloved husband said. "That music can't be far away. It's getting late. I don't want to be out here after dark."

Realizing the wisdom of his words I lugged myself to my feet and started after him. I still wondered where the rescuing people-mover was.

Walking in the deep sand was not easy, especially when I was wearing flip-flops, but the sand was blistering hot, so I couldn't go barefoot. Van is five-inches shorter than I am, but he really can cover the ground. He was clipping along while I struggled to keep my shoes on. Finally I yelled out to him to slow down a little. My long legs couldn't keep up with his short ones. I tried not to think about how far we had to go or how far we already had walked. I just concentrated on putting one foot in front of the other and plugged away. At one point we did meet a people-mover heading toward us. We were thrilled, but for the first time, we encountered a Brazilian that didn't have time to help us. Best we could understand was that he was going to the highway on his last trip and had to get his passengers on their way ASAP. He didn't have time to rescue stranded strangers. What a disappointment! He continued in the direction of our truck. We kept walking the other way. Then we encountered a fork in the road. We listened diligently to try to decide which way was toward the music. Two small boys carrying sacks on their backs approached. We did our best to ask them for directions, but obviously they never had seen people such as us. They were too awed to understand us; we surely couldn't understand them. With their eyes bulging and their mouths gaping they backed away from us, so we ended up just picking a road and going. We trudged along. Before we finally arrived, I really was beginning to get tired and frustrated.

On arrival what we found was a wide expanse of water with a town visible on the other side. We stopped and stared. We tried to figure out how to surmount this latest obstacle. The water wasn't a river or a creek; this was an ocean inlet. We didn't know how deep the water was. We didn't see any bridges. How were we supposed to get to town on the other side? As we watched, our question was answered. We saw some people wading across from the town toward us. Then a people-mover passed us going into town.

The truck went straight into the water and across. I wasn't too tired to register the fact that the truck was a people-mover. *Now the thing shows up. Thanks a lot!*

Van is not a water enthusiast. In fact his idea of a water sport is a shower. I knew he wasn't keen on the idea of wading across this unfamiliar stretch of water, but this time he had no choice. I struck out in the lead. Long legs are handy in water crossings. I really didn't want to get my clothes wet, so I hiked my pants leg as high as possible so I could work my way gingerly across the water. Van cautiously followed behind. We succeeded in crossing without plunging into the depths. However, once we were on the other side, we still were in a quandary about which way to go. We definitely could hear the sound cars, but what we actually could see were just a couple of houses with a "street" that led away from the water. But, hey, we were getting really good at just following our noses. In fact I was beginning to believe our noses were better than a GPS was. At random we picked a route and continued walking.

To me this place didn't look like a tourist destination. Even though I love nature, I couldn't imagine why anyone would choose this place to spend his or her vacation. We finally found an actual town—a fairly large town, all things considered. At the end of a street to our right we saw the sign for a mechanic and headed that way, where we hoped to find help. Just as we started up the street, I poked Van and said, "Hey! Look!" Yep, on the corner was the First Baptist Church of Santo Amaro. I've seen some beautiful churches in my time, but I'm not sure I've ever seen one that looked better than that one. Seeing it meant this trip to Santo Amaro would be our only one.

At the mechanic's shop we had a little trouble making ourselves understood. Obviously the people there were at the end of their workday and would really have preferred to go home rather than help two yoyos who hadn't known better than to try to drive here without their help in the first place. After we finally got our message across, one of the guys agreed to help us. He was a people-mover driver. Even though he had just gotten home, we hopped into his truck and headed back. This was really getting old.

He seemed to know exactly where our truck was. I suppose the place at which we got stuck was the only bad place between this town and the highway. *Who knew?* I noticed that when we reached the place, he didn't even drive the people-mover down into the little dip in which the SUV was snuggled.

When they saw our truck, the first thing the guys suggested was to use its wench. We were embarrassed to tell them that we didn't have its control. In that case, they told us, we needed to let some air out of the tires. Lowering the air pressure allows the tires to spread out and go across the sand easier. I found some fingernail clippers to use as a tool. I was handing them over to Van when I dropped them. Fortunately I was watching as they hit the sand, because they disappeared into the sand as if the sand were water. If I had not been watching, they would have been gone for good. That's how deep and soft the sand was.

The guys lowered the air pressure and tried driving the truck out, but that didn't work. Then they decided to pull the cable off the wench and use that to tow us out. *Who needed a stinking old control?* They hooked the cable to their truck and gave a good tug. Their truck skittered around on top of the sand as though it was a big bird on ice, but after a few seconds the SUV was free. Our helper told us that he would drive our truck on to town. Since he obviously was more accustomed to things here in Sand World, that suited us just fine. His buddy drove his truck. As we zipped along through the sand, we realized that if we hadn't gotten stuck, our situation could have been much worse. When we got to the water that we had to cross to get into town, we wouldn't have had any idea where to cross. I was considering this when the driver slammed on the brakes.

"*Disastre!*" he exclaimed as he leaped out.

Disaster? What disaster? Just when I thought the day's excitement was over, we had new developments. Up ahead the Bandeirante had run off the road. The truck had gone up a little embankment and into a tree. *How on earth had that happened?* He wasn't even going fast. I didn't think this was exactly a disaster, but the event surely wasn't good. Our helper/driver jumped out of our truck and into his. He threw the thing into reverse. I thought he was going to run right into us. That might have been a *disastre!* However, he narrowly missed us and pulled up on the road ahead. His friend was a new driver. I guess the thrill of being behind the wheel became too much for him. Somehow in the curve in the road he had lost control. Thankfully the truck was undamaged. Everything was OK. The *disastre!* was averted.

Although our helper clearly was upset, he still had our welfare in mind. He took us to a *pousada* and told us he would meet us in the morning to help us back across the water. We were only too happy to agree to that plan. We knew that crossing the water in the wrong place truly could be a *disastre!*

The next morning we loitered around on the beach while we waited for the man. We enjoyed watching the people go about their daily business. We saw entering from the highway the people-movers loaded to the brim with people. I again wondered why none had passed by us when we were stuck. I guess we had taken a wrong turn. That wasn't difficult to do in a sand-covered wilderness with no signs.

Our help arrived and took over. Instead of plunging directly into the water he turned around and backed across. That would keep the water from rushing into the engine and causing serious damage. The water at which he crossed rose at least up to the top of the wheel wells. The helper didn't just get us across and dump us on the other side. He insisted on driving us all the way out to the highway. Before he bid us goodbye, he made sure we got the tires inflated to the proper highway pressure. He truly was a Good Samaritan in Brazilian's clothing.

Chapter 19

Through the Lençois

We had learned our lesson well. Even though we were getting to be old hands at being stuck, that was not our idea of fun. After we went to Humberto do Campo, we decided to do the prudent thing. We decided to go back to Barreirinhas and hire Raimundo to guide us across the *Pequenos Lençóis* (Little Sheets) to Paulino Neves. Raimundo had been born in Paulino Neves, so we believed he knew the way. When we happened on the inevitable crossroads, he would know which way to turn. Having Raimundo as a guide would take the pressure off. We could enjoy the scenery. We had heard that the Lençóis was full of exotic scenery and wildlife. Maybe if we drove right through its middle, we would see some.

Entering Barreirinhas this time was much different than was our first trip to the place. To begin with, we entered from the opposite direction; we followed a paved road all the way. Seeing things we recognized was a pleasant experience. We drove past the now-familiar Baptist church. Then we passed our favorite restaurant and drove on down to the Pousada Boa Vista. With enthusiasm we greeted Enzo and his wife. We were happy to see them. They seemed as glad to see us as if we were old friends. They even put us back in "our" room. While we ate supper, we told them a little about our adventure in Santo Amaro. Then we explained that we wanted to hire Raimundo as a guide. Enzo called him so we could make arrangements. We planned to meet Raimundo at 8 the next morning. We then retired to our room for the night.

Raimundo was right on time. We were ready to go, so we got off to a good start. The price Raimundo was asking

148

seemed a little high to us. After all, we had driven from Tutoias to Paulino Neves. We had an idea in our mind of what the road would be like. However, Raimundo assured us that from here to Paulino Neves was *longe* (a long way.) He looked so pitiful that we decided to pay what he was asking and consider the payment a charitable contribution—something akin to a large tip. He hopped into the front seat. I took my place in the rear. Van, of course, was driving. We started off confidently on our little journey of 35 kilometers. We were downright lighthearted. After we had traveled in unknown territory, trusted our own devices, and gotten stuck more than once, having someone along who knew the way was reassuring.

Sure enough, the road soon turned into something less than a road; then all semblance of a road disappeared. In every direction all we could see was sand and scrubby growth. The gaps through the brushy trees and some vague tire tracks were our only indications that someone could drive through here. My feelings of confidence began to evaporate when Raimundo scooted up to the edge of the seat and began glancing around anxiously. He had made this trip many times in his life, but he never had driven this way. He didn't even know how to drive, but he gamely issued directions. Without question Van followed his instructions. In reality what else could he do? The sand was that deep stuff that sucked the tires in like a big puddle of glue. Stopping to discuss things was not an option. If we stopped, we stayed. We didn't want to do that again.

"That way," Raimundo said as he flung his hand to the left.

Van jerked the wheel; we swerved to the left and plunged along.

"Through there!" Raimundo said as he waved to the right.

We were fairly flying along. Van couldn't take the time to consider the directions. We had to keep moving as we drove through the deep sand.

"The truck's beginning to get hot," Van said. In horror I gaped at the temperature gauge. I did not want to trek across the Lençois! I looked around desperately for some firm stopping point we could reach so the truck could cool off. As usual all I saw was sand.

I never had understood people's fascination with sand. Many advertisements intended to lure one to the beach show a girl wearing a bikini and a big hat as she sits on top of a lonely dune and gazes wistfully off across the ocean as she tries to make everyone jealous. Those advertisements are lost on me. What little attraction I had had for sand quickly swirled down the drain. At this point I didn't care if I never saw another sand dune!

Trying his best to ignore the truck's rising temperature, Van, too, was searching for a place to stop. We didn't find a resting place, but we did find water.

Oh, boy! What fun we're having! I thought.

Fortunately the sand near the water was pretty solid, so we were able to stop. Raimundo hopped out and waded out into the water. I knew he was checking to see whether the water was too deep to cross. Seeing him hike his pant legs up was not encouraging. For some reason water crossings such as this now made me nervous. I never used to be like that.

And, I thought, *what if the water is too deep? What do we do then?*

I looked around me. Prospects didn't seem too bright. After a few minutes Raimundo walked back to us. He told us we could cross the water. I was so excited. This was just what I was looking for today—more adventure. Van and Raimundo got back into the truck. Prayers rose heavenward. Van put the truck into gear and plunged in. Steam boiled up over the windshield; the glass fogged up. We couldn't see a thing ahead of us, but we didn't stop. The motor kept running; we exited on the other side. All of us were trembling.

Even Raimundo knew that putting the hot engine into that cold water could be a major problem. Once we were completely out of the water on the far side, we stopped again. Van raised the hood to see what damage had been done. Lots of steam billowed out, but, praise God, once again we had managed to cross the water safely. We paused long enough to regroup. Then we were off again. We were relieved to be across the water, but not much else had changed. The landscape looked the same as it had before. Soon the truck again was on the verge of getting too hot. We still were sand-surfing.

Then suddenly we happened onto a real road. Well, at the time the thing looked like a *real road*. To most people the road would have been considered a horrible, rutted, dirt track that was bumpy and rough. To us this road looked as though it was an oasis in the desert. Its solid surface was the one thing we really were glad to see. Raimundo grinned. Van sighed. I sat back and almost cried. I was so glad to have that safely behind us. I don't know what on earth led me to think everything would be OK now.

The better road made a huge difference. Now that the SUV wasn't struggling through deep sand, the truck began to cool off. I looked out the windows and searched the Lençois for the beauty I had heard about. Guess what I saw? That's right . . . sand. Sand, sand, and more sand. I thought about the bathing beauty in her bikini and broad-brimmed beach hat as she might have perched atop one of these dunes. I couldn't imagine how she would get up on the dune or why she would want to in the first place. What I did know was that she could have my share of sand dunes. I just wanted to get out of this place!

We had heard that the Lençois was supposed to have all kinds of exotic birds. I didn't even see a *bem-ti-vi*, a common bird that I considered the Brazilian equivalent of a blue jay. I did take advantage of the smoother road and snapped a few pictures. I wasn't thrilled to be here, but for later I wanted proof that I had been. I wasn't planning on passing this way again.

A long time later we passed a house. *Amazing! Someone lived out here.* That someone wanted a ride out of here. I could understand that. Contrary to our normal aversion to picking up strangers we stopped for him. I wasn't keen on leaving anyone out here, even if he did call the place *home.* Our new passenger was a taciturn fellow. That suited me just fine. Just then I surely wasn't in the mood to launch into a happy little conversation in Portuguese. I was feeling very emotionally drained. I sat back and stared out the window.

Raimundo was supposed to be our guide, I thought bitterly. *He was supposed to take us straight through to Paulino Neves without problems.*

Then a thought occurred to me. *What if we hadn't had Raimundo? We never would have found our way through here. This was nothing like the road from Tutoias to Paulino Neves.* I looked around again. I thought about wandering aimlessly until we could go no farther before we collapsed and died out in this forbidding wasteland. Years later someone would find a few of our sun-bleached bones. That would be all that was left of us. Then I thanked God for Raimundo.

At last, after what seemed as though it was lifetime, we got to Paulino Neves. I had forgotten what a beautiful town this little burg was. We pulled up to the bus station and paid Raimundo his well-earned fee. Before he would leave us, he had to be satisfied that from here we could manage on our own. Like most of the Brazilians we had met, once he signed on to help us, he considered us his responsibility until he was convinced we were safely delivered to our destination. Now we were safely delivered. I was badly shaken but safely delivered as I waved goodbye to our new friend.

Chapter 20

Where in the World Is Alcântara?

We were approaching the end our mapping research. Our plan now was to go the western border of the State of Maranhão and to work our way back to Fortaleza. We knew this would be one of our last excursions. We were praying that the SUV would be able to make the trip.

Driving across the huge State of Maranhão took three days. We spent one night with our friends, Vic and Sharon, in Parnaiba and another one at a hotel between São Luis and our destination, Carutapera. When we finally reached the place, we were not impressed. The town was bustling with people; since election time was near, sound cars were everywhere.

In many parts of Brazil the sound cars politicians use to promote their causes are outlawed, while other places allow them. Evidently Carutapera was one of the places that allowed them. Apparently the good people of Carutapera loved their sound cars, because they had plenty of them stalking the streets. Then, just to add to the confusion, at 6 p.m. the Catholic church began broadcasting a service from the loud-speakers in its bell tower. The service began with Gounod's *Ave Maria*. A sermon followed.

The *pousada* we located was clean. That's about the only good thing I can say about the place. The next morning we slept in until 6 a.m. That is when the Catholic church awakened us with a repeat of the last night's performance.

After our acceptable breakfast Van discovered that the SUV needed two quarts of oil. All day the day before, the truck had been smoking as though it were a chimney and whining as though it were a kicked puppy. The repair job that was supposed to be just the ticket and took six months to complete had turned out to be not so hot. That was a major disappointment, because we had such high hopes for this vehicle. *Oh well!* We did know some good mechanics.

In spite of all the annoying things we encountered in Carutapera, we were happy to see a new Baptist church being built in the town. After we left Carutapera, we ducked into Goldofredo Viana. Then we drove to Candido Mendes. Both of these are large towns, so we didn't need to hang around. However, in Candido Mendes we saw a large Baptist church. Some people were working at the church, so we stopped in to visit with them. The pastor was very informative. He told us that his church and others in the area were working to evangelize the nearby islands. He said German missionaries working out of São Luis were helping them. This was very good news to us. Learning this meant we could leapfrog some of the areas we had planned to visit, because we already knew they had Baptist churches and ministries.

Our experiences with Brazilians had been so positive. As a rule they are warm, helpful people, but as we traveled westward in Maranhão, we encountered more suspicion. The people were more distant and less friendly. We attributed their attitude to the fact that they were more isolated; fewer foreigners passed through their towns. We saw more poverty in this part of the country, too. Many people live in small, wooden houses that had thatched roofs. That was a lot different from the other places we had seen. On top of that, the accent here was more difficult to understand.

Having finished our research we were ready to go back to Fortaleza. Of course to choose the best route we consulted the well-used map book. The book showed a town called Alcântara that was situated across the bay from São Luis. That seemed as though it would be a good place to spend the night, so we headed in that direction. The plan was to spend the night in Alcântara and to take the ferry across the bay in the morning. Since the time was the middle of the afternoon, we thought we were being reasonable to expect to arrive before dark. Why hadn't we yet learned that *seeming reasonable* and *being reasonable* were not the same thing?

We decided we still had time to check out a couple of more little towns before we went to Alcântara. Happily we found Baptist churches everywhere we went. The German Baptists from São Luis seemed to be doing an effective job.

As the daylight began to wane, we left the main road and drove toward Alcântara. We drove and drove. This town wasn't supposed to be that far off the highway. At least the road was paved and well-cared for. Well, the road was well-cared for until we passed a turnoff that had signs directing people to the ferry. After that the asphalt became patchy in some places and nonexistent in others.

Where on earth was Alcântara? We thought the ferry left from that town. As I've said before, we really tried to avoid driving after dark. Today we believed we had given ourselves plenty of time, but here we were after dark on this lonely stretch of road; we were unsure whether the town we sought would have lodgings for us. That particular scenario was wearing a little thin. To add to the gloom, literally, when Van turned on the headlights, they produced only an anemic little glimmer. (Surprise! Surprise!) We didn't even see any wildlife. For me that would have been a perk.

After what seemed an eternity, we saw some lights off in the distance across a field. Hope sprang up. After 20 or 30 more minutes, we got to the edge of the town. Another car now was in front of us. We followed that car through the dark, narrow streets and hoped the thing would lead us to the "hotel district." We weren't seeing any lodgings. The folks in front of us apparently were as lost as we were. They pulled over to the side of the street and spoke to some folks sitting on the corner.

We saw lots of waving of hands and nodding of heads. Then the car eased away down the street. We asked the same people for directions to a hotel. We got the same waves and nods. We, too, proceeded down the street and looked diligently for the sign we had been told we would see. Sure enough, we found a sign hanging above a door of what appeared to be just another house. But, hey! The sun had gone down and the hour was late. We didn't want to do any more exploring that day. We went in and asked for a room. Yes, they had vacancies. The clerk led us up a flight of well-worn stairs and around a corner to a huge wooden door that had great big strap hinges holding the door in place. Using an ancient-looking key he proudly swung the door open. We stepped in. The room was big and shabby with an even shabbier bathroom attached. I felt as though we had stepped back a hundred years in time. However, the room was clean; I thought staying in this hotel would be neat. Maybe the place was haunted.

We dragged our many pieces of luggage up the long flight of stairs and settled in. The place really was amazing. This hotel must be centuries old. We locked the door behind us, but the door had big gaps all the way around the frame. I wasn't afraid, but I thought that if anyone wanted to get into our room, that flimsy lock wouldn't stop a person.

The next morning I pulled back the curtains to see where we were. I was astounded to see the ocean not far away. Everything definitely looked better than it had the night before. We got dressed and went downstairs for breakfast. We were directed to a dining area at the bottom of the hotel and just off a small courtyard. The courtyard was covered with cracked tiles. A tall wall draped with blooming vines surrounded the patio. A great big well was in the middle of everything. An old man sat at the table at which *café da manha* was laid out. The waiter told us the man was descended from the original owners of the house. To me he looked to be as old as the

156

hotel was. While we ate, the old man told us some of the history of the hotel. The place was 250-years old. Originally this hotel had been the private residence of his grandfather. Later the home was transformed into a hotel. The landed and wealthy people of São Luis would send their spoiled br . . ., uh, children to the place for vacation before the kids went overseas to school.

After breakfast we had a wonderful time wandering around the town. Alcântara is an active town full of the historical ruins of old buildings and churches. Unfortunately the biggest church was in the process of being renovated. Through cracks in the fence we got only a peek of that one. Many places in town had spectacular views of the ocean. We were happy that we had stumbled into this town.

As we left town in the bright morning sunshine, the desolate drive of the previous evening didn't look so frightful. We didn't have any problem locating the turnoff to the ferry since we had passed by the road the night before. We got to the dock quite early, so we had to wait around for a long time.

This ferry was no little barge with a weedeater motor. This was a ship with several levels. After we boarded and got parked, we went up to a lounge on the top level. A lot of people were on this trip. Van had a book, but I spent my time looking out the windows and taking in the sights.

When we got to the other side, we were unceremoniously dumped into the city of São Luis. That was highly unnerving, since we never had been in this city before. We had no idea where we wanted to go, much less how to find the place. I was frantically looking at the map while Van struggled to avoid a crash. The traffic in this city was as crazy as it was in all large Brazilian cities. We decided that the beach would be our best bet to quickly find a good place to stay. With our map we could find the beach, so that's where we went.

We found a good beach with plenty of nice, modern, tourist-friendly places to stay. We even encountered some people who spoke English . . . or who at least thought they did. I loved the beach in São Luis. The beach had a "boardwalk" with people meandering around. A row of restaurants was across the street from our hotel. This looked as though it might be a nice place to spend a couple of days before we headed home. The trip back to Fortaleza still was a long way.

Getting out of São Luis proved to be as challenging as getting into the town had been. For a long time we drove in circles before we found the highway out of the city. When we finally found the road, we were back in familiar territory. We were happy actually to know where we were going again, but we had enjoyed our latest foray into the unknown.

Chapter 21

Leaving Fortaleza

Our year working on the coast had been unbelievable. We started off way down at the southern end of Bahia and had worked our way all the way over to Maranhão. We had found places that had lots of Baptist work. We had seen places that had none. We had located villages that didn't have churches at all as well as towns that had many. We had reached the western border of our assignment. The mapping job that had brought us to Brazil was completed. Now we needed to find a new job.

God blessed us by allowing us to choose the place in which we would like to work. We considered several options. I thought I would like to work in the jungle areas near the Amazon. We checked into some jobs in that part of the country. Then we checked out the average daily temperatures in that part of the county. Then we decided to look elsewhere.

Nolen, the regional leader, suggested a town in the State of Minas Gerais. For many years he had worked in the northeast part of Brazil, where Minas Gerais was situated, so the area was dear to his heart. We decided to visit the town. An experienced colleague went with us. That was how, after much prayer and discussion, we decided to move to Diamantina, Minas Gerais. No American missionaries had served in that historic town.

This job would be very different from what we had been doing. We would be working in the area of church planting. That meant we would be working directly with Brazilian nationals. In the new job we would be using our Portuguese a lot more. The state capital, Belo Horizonte, in which missionaries David and Laurie lived, was 500 kilometers away. They would be our closest IMB contacts.

Since we now were old pros at moving and traveling, we wanted to drive from Fortaleza to our new home. We had seen a lot of the coast. We wanted to explore a little of the interior, too. Besides, driving would be the cheapest way for us to move. We would have to ship some of our stuff, but we could take things with us as well.

The first order of business was to pack (that's always such fun). Then, to await our arrival, we would ship to David and Laurie much of what we had. Packing was a familiar chore, but then we had to take the baggage to the air-freight office for shipping. Using our Portuguese to make all the arrangements with the woman at the freight company was a bit of a challenge, but we managed to get the job done. Once those details were settled, we were ready to begin our journey.

Our route would take us across the desert-like Sertão area of northeast Brazil. Even at the onset of the trip we were a little uneasy about crossing that dry, arid region in the undependable SUV. Its past behavior did not instill confidence in what its future behavior would be. The thing still wasn't running just right, even though everything was supposed to have been repaired. That SUV was a perfect object lesson for not judging things by outward appearances. Van thought if we babied the old truck along, we would be OK. I had my doubts, but we didn't see any point in taking the truck to the shop again. That hadn't worked in the past. We decided to just start driving and see what happened. We'd worry about repairs when we needed to worry about repairs.

On our first day out we didn't have any problems, so we were encouraged. On the second day . . . well, on the second day things were a little different. On that day we got into the edge of the Sertão. The truck began to complain by overheating. At first the problem was just a little one. We turned off the

AC and lowered the windows to see whether that would help, but the temperature continued to go up and up. Finally we knew we couldn't push the thing further without major problems. Plus we didn't want to be in a completely deserted area. We had just passed through a small town. We pulled to the side of the road to call Ed. As far as I was concerned, having to call Ed was a very major problem in itself. Ed must have been thrilled to death to hear from us again. Most of our phone calls to him were cries of help.

As we sat on the edge of the road, Van began to explain our situation to him. *Highway* is too dignified a term to use for the thoroughfare on which we sat. The big trucks that passed perilously close shook our truck and my nerves. I begged Van at least to go back to the last little burg we had passed to talk on the phone. At last he hung up and turned around.

"Ed suggested that we try to go back to Fortaleza and fly to Diamantina," Van explained.

Plan A, to drive to Diamantina, had crashed and burned, but to me Plan B sounded as though it was a horrible suggestion. Besides being disappointed I didn't think the truck would agree to this plan either, if you know what I mean. So I told Van my opinion.

"Well, I agree," he said, "but we'll at least try. We'll put more water in the radiator and see what happens."

Well, what happened is that we filled the radiator and started toward Fortaleza. Within five kilometers the truck began seriously overheating again. Back we went to the town, Barros. We enlisted the help of the *frentistas* (service-station attendants). They had a couple of suggestions, but those suggestions proved to be fruitless. In the end we went to the *oficina* (mechanic's shop). The people there took a look and then took the truck for a test-drive. When they returned, they told us that they thought they could fix the problem in an hour or two. We were elated but not very optimistic.

Fortunately a good place to eat was right next to the shop, so while we were waiting, we had lunch. A deaf man walked through the restaurant and asked for donations. He was selling rosary beads, little crucifixes, and stickers for children. He put a rosary on the table, placed on top of that his card explaining that he was deaf, and grinned at me. When I left the truck, I had grabbed a handful of tracts. I looked at the rosary and his card. On top of that I laid a tract that looked as though it was a trump card and grinned back. He picked up the tract. I picked up some of the stickers and gave him a couple of *reis* (the Brazilian equivalent of a dollar). He walked away reading the tract. You never know when a seed you plant might sprout.

Do I really have to tell you that the efforts of the guys at the mechanic shop were in vain? I mean, you saw that headed in our direction, didn't you? After doing their best, they told us — surprise, surprise — that the head gasket was blown! Again! After all that time, effort, and money to send the truck to Brasilia for repairs, here we sat with the same old problem. To say the least we were dismayed. We went back to the drawing board to develop Plan C. The new plan was to haul the truck to the dealership in the larger town of Juazeiro do Norte to see whether the dealership could get the thing up and going again. Juazeiro do Norte had not been on our initial itinerary, but we let the mechanic make arrangements for the dealership to pick up the truck the next morning. I'm sure Ed groaned when he saw our number on the caller-ID portion of his phone. He had to know the call could be only more bad news.

Since we were going to be staying overnight, we had to find a place to stay. We were not surprised to learn that this little spot in the road didn't have lots of options for lodging. We settled on a little hole-in-the-wall place. Literally. From ground level the only indication of the *pousada* level was a doorway that led to the main quarters on the second floor. The room was a shabby little area, but the place was very clean and was off the street.

The next morning we walked back to the mechanic's shop. The people there told us the tow truck wouldn't arrive for another couple of hours, so we settled in to wait. Waiting is a good exercise to develop patience. These days we were developing lots of patience. Good for me I am easily amused. I dragged out my crossword puzzle book and set to work.

The wrecker finally arrived. The operator began to load our truck. I was on the sidewalk near a man with a donkey cart. I was struck by the realization that the donkey cart was a more reliable source of transportation than was our fancy motor vehicle.

Once the truck was on the wrecker, the driver, Van, and I piled in for the trek to Juazeiro. The trip was agonizingly slow. Our driver was cheerful and talkative, but talkative is not so good when you can understand only bits and pieces of what the guy is saying. We really couldn't carry on a conversation. Although by this time we were communicating pretty well in Portuguese, the accents in different parts of the country complicated things. The driver told us that he would take us by his house before going to the dealership so we could get some water . . . not that we wanted water. I think he wanted to show off his new American "friends." We were probably the first Americans he had met. After the water stop we went on to the car place. Making arrangements for getting the truck repaired once again was another challenge. At last things were more or less settled. Someone from the shop took us to find a hotel. Apparently we might be waiting for a while. Patience is a virtue, so they say.

All of this happened right at Thanksgiving time. Of course, Thanksgiving isn't a national holiday in Brazil, but on that day many American missionaries get together to thank God for His goodness. We weren't really happy about being stuck in

Juazeiro do Norte all by ourselves. To add insult to injury, when we talked to Ed, he regaled us with the story of his delicious Thanksgiving dinner. Maybe he was getting us back for interrupting him. Regardless, we had walked all around the town near the hotel and hadn't even been able to find a good restaurant. We decided to go back to the hotel to have lunch. We ordered a pizza. Pizza is very popular in Brazil. Brazilian pizza, although not like the American version, is usually very good. Usually. When the waiter delivered the pizza to our table, he began to serve us, as is the custom in Brazil. Brazilian waiters normally use a pair of spoons or forks in a manner sort of like chopsticks to lift the food to your plate. This waiter struggled and struggled to get a piece of the pie. At last he grabbed one, but as he went to put the pizza on my plate, the pizza flipped over and fell back onto the pan.

"I don't believe this," he muttered to himself.

After a prolonged struggle he finally was successful in depositing a piece of pizza on my plate. Then he dropped the utensils on the tray and stalked off without even considering serving Van. We had to laugh.

The pizza was absolutely the worst pizza I have ever eaten in my life. The crust was like thick cardboard, so we scraped the toppings off and ate them. They were less than delicious. This made us even more envious of Ed. This truly was a Thanksgiving dinner we would not forget.

The next day when we talked to the people at the car dealership, we realized we were going to be in Juazeiro for some time. The hotel we were in was quite a nice one, but we thought we could find a less-expensive place to stay. Finding a really nice hotel at a reasonable price didn't take long. We settled in for our unexpected vacation.

Meanwhile, back at the car dealership, things were not looking good for the home team. The first thing we were told was that the mechanics would have to order a part for the truck before they could even do the test to see what was wrong with the SUV. They would have to get the part from São Paulo. That would take a couple of days and would cost a couple hundred *reis*. We knew that getting the part was not necessary, but without doing that, Plan C, to get the truck repaired and continue on our way, was dead.

Hello, Ed. You got a Plan D?

We had to get the truck back to Brasilia for repairs—*ha ha*—or to be sold. Personally I thought finding a high cliff over which we could push the truck would be a good solution. However, working with Ed, we decided that Plan D would be to hire the same guy who had brought us to Juazeiro do Norte to take the truck on to Brasilia. When we told the man about our idea, he seemed to be eager to make the trip. He told Ed that he would need to get his documents in order first, but every time Ed talked to him, he kept saying he needed just another day or so. A day dragged on into two and then three. At last we determined that our friendly wrecker driver just didn't have the necessary documents. He couldn't haul the truck for us. *Hmm.* Guess we needed to think about Plan E. At least we liked our accommodations.

Uh, Ed, what are your thoughts about Plan E?

By this time we were really frustrated. We had been in Juazeiro do Norte for three days. We still were not sure how we were going to get out of the town, but since we were going to be here for at least another couple of days, we decided to make the best of the situation.

Juazeiro do Norte is the home of Padre Cicero. He was a Catholic priest who lived in the 19th century. In 1895 he supposedly wrought a miracle by causing blood in the form of the "sacred heart" to appear on the host he gave to an elderly woman during mass. For some reason he was excommunicated from the Church because of this miracle, but in the minds of many Brazilians he was elevated to the level of a saint. Some consider him a messiah who will turn the Sertão into an oasis. Later he became a political leader. The town has a gigantic, 75-foot-tall statue of the good father. The statue is surrounded by shops that sell "body parts" that can be bought for display in the shrine to represent the part of the supplicant's body that supposedly was healed by the saint. Each year many Brazilians make pilgrimages to Padre Cicero's tomb. To demonstrate their devotion they will walk long distances to get to the shrine. Many crawl the last part of the way, including up a long flight of stairs, to gain the padre's blessing. As we walked around the area dedicated to him, we were amazed at what people were willing to do to please and adore this man who had died so many years before. To his credit Padre Cicero himself did not claim to be super-human.

One good thing about being stuck in Juazeiro was that I could use our international phone. Every day I talked to our daughters, Nancy and Marci. The hotel had a good restaurant and a nice pool, but I have to admit we really didn't have much Christmas spirit as we sat around the pool in shorts while we watched the hotel personnel put lights on the nearby trees. At first, sitting by the pool while we read our Bibles in the mornings was pleasant, but as the days dragged by, we began to get anxious.

Our latest plan was to figure out a way to get our truck and us to Brasilia. Once in Brasilia we would get another vehicle, since this one appeared to be mortally wounded. Then the beloved SUV no longer would be our problem. Ed was working on making these arrangements. We were just waiting for a call from him. Finally we got the call. Ed had found someone to haul the SUV to Brasilia. All we had to do was make connections with that person. Then we would fly to Brasilia.

Back we went to the dealership where the SUV waited. More mumble-jumble in Portuguese. More waiting. Finally, after 6 in the evening the wrecker arrived to take the truck across town to another place to be picked up in a day or two for the trip to Brasilia. The truck still was full of our stuff. We could take only some of the things with us. We would have to trust the people moving the truck to transport our stuff, too. We gathered a few of the most important things.

Ed had booked a flight for us from Juazeiro to Brasilia. The next morning we took a taxi to the airport. While we were in Fortaleza, we had learned the fine art of using a taxi. Too bad we hadn't had that skill when we were in Salvador. Being familiar with taxis would have been useful in that city.

The airport was a big surprise. I guess we had been expecting an airport such as the one in Fortaleza. We forgot that Juazeiro was tiny in comparison to Fortaleza. This airport was not nearly as big and nice as the bus station in Recife was. The airport had one ticket window and one waiting room. When we arrived, only a few people were hanging around. We got our tickets without a problem and waited at the only gate. The waiting area was a large room with floor-to-ceiling windows that looked out onto the tarmac. The runways had no fences around them. Near the building the planes were parked as though they were cars. I guess the pilots just drove up to the door and got out.

As the room began to fill up, we began to get nervous. This flight seemed to have a lot of people. Being Brazilians, everyone was talking to everyone else. The room was very noisy. Then a woman entered and shouted out an announcement about a flight. Since the room had no PA system, we could barely hear her. We understood only a little of what she said. Many of the people began filing out the door and walking toward a plane. A few minutes later she made another announcement; more people started leaving. So many more people were leaving, we were afraid we were missing our flight. We asked someone near us what flight number she had called. He confirmed our fears. We wove anxiously through the crowd and thrust our tickets under the woman's nose just as she was closing the door to the tarmac.

"Yes, this is your flight! Hurry before they close the door on the airplane!" she said as she flung her door open.

So we hurried. We raced across the tarmac and up the steps to the back door. We squeaked in; the plane's door closed behind us. *That had been close.*

We flew from Juazeiro do Norte to Belo Horizonte. In Belo we had to get off the plane and check in through security again. We rushed into the terminal and began searching for the gate we needed. Unlike the airport in Juazeiro the one in Belo Horizonte is very big. Fortunately we had flown to Belo when we had made our trip to Diamantina. We weren't completely lost. The gate we sought was upstairs at the other end of the airport. We dashed down the corridor not quite like O.J. did in those old commercials, but almost. This time Van was the one who was anxious. He kept looking at his watch and fretting about missing our connection. He breathed a huge sigh of relief when at last we found the gate. However, we had just cleared the security inspection when his anxiety returned. We were not at the right gate after all. We zipped back through security and farther down the corridor. We fidgeted while the security people did their thing. Once past them we hurried over to the gate. Imagine our shock when we saw the sign that directed us back to the gate we had just left! Van was nearly frantic. He is the kind of person who always is on time. Missing this connection would be disturbing to him. Once more we flew back down the corridor and through security. I wondered what those people thought of us. At last we were where we needed to be. When we relaxed enough to breathe again, we walked over toward the window that overlooked the runways. Our plane was waiting for boarding. Van's jaw dropped. The plane we had scrambled to find was the same one from which we had just disembarked! When we went on board to continue our journey, we walked down the aisle and seated ourselves in the same seats we had vacated about a half-hour earlier.

When we touched down in Brasilia, Ed and his wife, Deborah, were waiting for us. We were happy to surrender to their thoughtful care.

Chapter 22

A Place of Our Own

The headquarters for our mission is in Brasilia, the capital of the country. At one time this beautiful complex had lots of activity. Now, only a few folks work at this office, but the place still is the hub of the mission. Until further developments we would be staying at the guest house. The house was gigantic compared to our tiny little apartment in Fortaleza.

Brasilia is situated in the exact geographical center of the country in its own federal district. Imagine the capital of the United States being somewhere in Kansas. The city was designed and built specifically as the governing city. Before Brasilia was built, Rio de Janeiro had the capital of Brazil. In 1956 work began on building the new capital. To me, the place is a little Orwellian . . . you know, *1984*. The city is divided into sections for work, sections for living, sections for shopping, etc. Brasilia is not like Brazil. If someone visits only this city, he or she will not get a true picture of the country. I think the idea of having the capital in the center of the country is interesting but in reality is not very practical. The city is facing some problems now because the population of the city has far outgrown its design. On top of that the surrounding suburbs have mushroomed too.

We had made some progress by finally getting out of the Sertão, but we were still a long, long way from Diamantina. Our venture was not over yet. The first thing we had to do was to get another vehicle. This would make at least four vehicles that the mission had assigned to us.That is not counting all the ones we had driven while our assigned one was being repaired. We had the opportunity to get a new car, but we were concerned that the horrible streets in Diamantina and the dirt roads in the surrounding areas would ruin it. We decided on another SUV. This one didn't have four-wheel drive, but we were hoping we wouldn't need that much anymore.

The next thing we needed to do was to get all of our stuff in one place. Part of our stuff was with us; part was in Belo Horizonte, and a third part was still in our SUV in Juazeiro do Norte or somewhere between there and Brasilia. The logical thing to do seemed to be to wait in Brasilia until the SUV arrived. That would be about a week, according to the people shipping the truck. *Why were we inclined to doubt that?* Meanwhile, we learned more about Brasilia. We also got to spend quality time with Ed. He really is a great guy (so great, in fact, that I asked him to write one of the forewords to this book—for his kind words see page 13).

We waited that week for our truck, but, just as we suspected, we waited in vain. We were stir-crazy and eager to be on our way. We had left Fortaleza more than two weeks earlier. Finally we couldn't wait any longer. We decided to strike out for Diamantina with or without our worldly goods. We would just have to return to get them some day.

Twenty days after leaving Fortaleza we arrived in Diamantina. The trip should have taken about three days. Even though our things still were scattered in three cities, we were delighted to finally reach our destination. We stopped at the first hotel we saw. The clerk showed us a room with a spa tub. *Wow,* what a luxury a long soak in the tub would be. That clinched the deal. We told her we would stay. Van signed the long check-in form and gave the form to the clerk. That's when she explained that we would have to use the shower since the spa tub didn't work. I was deflated. I guess the tub was just window-dressing.

After one night in the place with the non-working spa tub, we moved to another hotel in the center part of the city. Then we spent some time exploring our new hometown. After a while we got hungry, so we ducked into a handy place to eat. The owner of the restaurant, Xavier, could speak a few words of English. He was eager to demonstrate for us. What a character he was. He was unkempt and smelled of alcohol. His shirt was open about halfway down the front. Soon I picked up on the cool relationship between him and a woman I finally identified as his wife. At the time none of us had a clue about the impact we would have on each other. Diamantina is full of restaurants. We could have picked any number of other places to eat that day, but we picked the P X 4.

Now that we were in Diamantina, we thought our days as vagabonds were over. We thought finding a place to live would be simple. We were wrong again! Unfortunately, we had arrived at quite possibly the worst time of the year: just before Carnaval. Once again the crazy celebration was going to throw a major crimp in our plans. For some odd reason this small, historic town attracts to it throngs of people for Carnaval. Many of the locals cash in on this by renting their houses for the week. In that week they can make as much money as they would make in a whole year of "normal" rental. This was bad news for us, because all of the nice houses already were rented.

When Xavier found we were looking for a place to rent, he assumed the role of real-estate agent. He told us to return later in the afternoon so he could show us around and help us look for a house. We were a little nervous about the idea. Even though we had lived in Brazil for nearly two years, we had not had the chance to develop many close friendships with Brazilians. However, we knew we needed to begin working on this, so we agreed to meet him.

Xavier's car was a tiny, two-door sedan. I left the shotgun seat for Van and folded myself into the back seat. The streets in Diamantina are cobbled and steep, so you rarely get out of second gear. That meant we basically crawled around town as we looked for houses. Xavier would see someone he knew on the street. He would stop and say, "These are my American friends. They are looking for a nice house with a garage," but we had no luck in finding such a place to rent. For several days in a row we made these excursions but got no results.

A few days later we met Joessé, the pastor of a Baptist church in Diamantina. Joessé had a different circle of friends than Xavier did. He took us to other places, but we had no luck with him either. Meanwhile, we were trying to find a place ourselves by checking with local real-estate agents. Amazingly, in spite of the efforts of our well-meaning new friends, we were the ones who finally found a suitable apartment. We had found the place, but we were sure glad that Joessé was available to help us with the details. He was our Gilson in Diamantina. Ed helped out via Internet, but this time he didn't make the trip to approve our living quarters.

We spent another two weeks in the hotel. Christmas arrived and passed. Via computer we celebrated another long-distance holiday with our daughters. Finally as the year drew to a close, we began moving into our new home. At last we hung up our wanderers' boots. We had a place of our own.

Chapter 23

The Lesson of the Map Book

Our mapping job was done. We had covered a lot of ground and seen lots of things we never would see again. Now once more we would be packing up and moving. I would miss our life as nomads. That kind of life certainly had been interesting. God had used us in a most unusual way. Now the way was better prepared for others to go to these areas to share the gospel with the unreached people.

As I began to pack, many memories flooded my mind. The piece of whalebone Van had found on one of our earliest excursions. The sand dollars I had picked up a quarter of a mile from shore during low tide. The little knick-knacks I had bought as souvenirs. And, of course, the pictures. I picked up the worn map book on which we had depended so much as we traveled. I remembered buying the book in Campinas before we even finished language school. We knew we couldn't just strike out trusting only our instincts and following our noses. We would have to have something to guide us every day. We had just sort of stumbled across this particular book while we were looking for something else. The minute we saw this book, we knew it would be just the ticket. We had chosen wisely; the book had served us well. Now the cover was torn. The pages were bent and folded in places. The book had picked up smudges and smears during its journey. Notes were scribbled in various places. The fact that we had used that book a lot showed in its condition.

I opened the book and looked at the routes I had marked to help us remember all the places we had been. Then I clasped the book close to my heart and reflected on those places. Even

174

though on occasion we had gotten off-track, without this book we never would have found some of those locations. We would have not had any idea where to go.

My thoughts drifted from this book to another book—a book much more precious and valuable than this old map book. Of course, I was thinking about the Bible. That book is a Map Book for our lives. We need the Bible to guide us daily. The Bible is like an owner's manual that the Manufacturer has issued for people. Not using the Bible to show us where to go would be like Van and me taking off up the coast of Brazil with nothing more than happy thoughts. We had been in some places in which the map was no help—places such as the vast sand dunes of the Lençois National Park in Maranhão. There, without any guidance, we had to choose which way to go. Being in those places made me very anxious. When we ended up in those situations, I worried about what lay ahead and what would happen to us. I wondered whether we ever would find our way home. Being lost in a wilderness is scary, but being lost in the sand dunes of life without a guide is worse. Praise God, when we encounter crossroads in life, we can count on the Truest Book of all to give us direction. That Book will lead us down the right road—the road that leads home.

We don't have to worry or be anxious or afraid, because we truly are not alone. God has promised never to leave us nor forsake us. Few people would start out on a journey such as the one Van and I made without a map and some instructions. How amazing that many people undertake the journey of life without the Bible!

What does your Bible look like? Is yours shiny and fresh as it was the day you bought the book? Are the pages pristine? Well, your Bible shouldn't look that way! Open that Book. Read its instructions. Make notes. Dwell in its pages. Drink from the Water of Life you will find in that Book. Rely on the Guide. Use that Book. Your life won't be without wrong turns and dead ends, but you'll never be lost. In the Book you can find how to get to the City on a Hill. You can look in the Book and see that He has prepared a place for you. You can rest in the assurance that He will show you how to get to that place.

Photo Album

A coconut grove near Conde, Bahia

The SUV after we
finally got it on the
wrecker in Conde,
Bahia

Sandro, our taxi-
driver and helper
when we broke
down in Conde

Van takes a little break.

Eucalyptus trees such as these are grown in many parts of Brazil.

An inland village in northeastern Seregipe

Sometimes we went to great heights to talk to people.

The moonlight on the water looked beautiful from the window of the Pousada Recanto do Pontal in Coruripe, Alagoas.

Horses are quite handy. These carts were used to collect the catch from the boats in Pontal do Peba.

Driving on the beach at Pontal do Peba, Alagoas

Repair time

Boats in the sea at Lagoa Azeda, Alagoas

This was the first cashew I ever saw on a tree. Brazilians enjoy the fruit, too.

Van with our new friend Juca and his wife in Pacatuba, Seregipe

The beach in Mucuri

We drove for miles down this muddy road going to Costa Dourada.

The bleak beach in Costa Dourada, Bahia

Burro and friend

Fabio cutting Van's hair in
Cumuruxatiba, Bahia

The balsa ticket office in
which the people let me
use their restroom

When Van can do this, we
know God is at work.

One brick at a time, this man is patiently building a street.

Boats on the beach in Canoa Quebrada

We were surprised to see the Baptist church on Broadway Street in Canoa Quebrada.

Welcome to Galinhos, Rio Grande do Norte. These are the mule-cart taxis used on this island on which the people don't have cars.

Kicking back in Galinhos after a long, tough day

The room at Pousada do Pisassal in Galinhos—not the nicest place we stayed, but the owner was very gracious.

Going down the beach in a mule cart

A section of this road, below, had been washed out by flooding. For two hours we wandered in the wilderness trying to detour around.

Below, the lighthouse in Galinhos

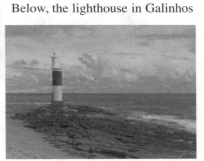

This balsa was just big enough to hold our truck. The man used a pole to push us across the water.

Since we couldn't get a picture of ourselves, we took pictures of each other (at right).

Looks like fun!

Muddin'!

At left, this is the road through the woods in Rio Grande do Norte. That day we drove through this type of stuff for many miles without seeing anyone.

The one picture I managed to get when we were stuck on the beach in Rio Grande do Norte

A foundering boat in Touros, Rio Grande do Norte

The people in Sucatinga were eager to talk to us. This man at right shows off his recent catch.

Converted beach bums, left

A boat on the beach in the Delta

On our way to Barreirinhas we passed this scenic water crossing before the road got bad.

The road going to Barreirinhas did get bad. In some places it was just barely wide enough for the truck.

Water is life.

Cajueiro—a grove of cashew trees on the northern coast of Brazil

When we were working west of Fortaleza, we often drove in sand such as this.

Going through the mangroves on our boat trip to Mandacaru and Atins

The beachfront restaurant at which we stopped when we worked from Barreirinhas

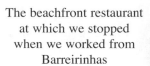

187

Van with the monkey
at the restaurant

Mandacaru, Maranhão

The lighthouse plaza in
Mandacaru

Too late to turn back now. We found
ourselves in that situation way too often.

A loaded "people-mover" in
Santo Amaro do Maranhão

This is the water crossing into Santo Amaro. The water is deeper than it looks.

Van and the SUV waiting for our helper in Santo Amaro

A group of huts in Maranhão

The Lençois in Maranhão is acres and acres of sand dunes.

Raimundo checking to see whether we can go through this water on our trip through the Lençois

189

Sand and shadows

A view of the Lençois
between Barreirinhas and
Paulino Neves

Wild cattle we saw while
we crossed the Pequena
Lençois with Raimundo

Diamantina, Minas Gerais, the town in
which we spent the last year of our term

190

To order more copies of
Misadventures in Travel

at $14.95 each plus shipping

Call us toll free:

1-800-747-0738

Mail $14.95 plus $4 shipping and handling for the first book (add $0.50 for each additional book):

Hannibal Books
P.O. Box 461592
Garland, TX 75046

Visit our website:

www.hannibalbooks.com

FAX us your order:
1-888-252-3022

Email us:
orders@hannibalbooks.com